the COMPL

dream book

of Love and Relationships

Discover What Your Dreams and Intuition
Reveal about You and Your Love Life

GILLIAN HOLLOWAY, PHD

sourcebooks
casablanca

Copyright © 2010 by Gillian Holloway
Cover and internal design © 2010 by Sourcebooks, Inc.
Cover design by Michel Vrana/Black Eye Design
Cover images © ZoneCreative/iStockphoto.com; Bastar/iStockphoto.com; Liliboas/iStockphoto.com

Published by Sourcebooks Casablanca, an imprint of Sourcebooks, Inc.
P.O. Box 4410, Naperville, Illinois 60567-4410
(630) 961-3900
Fax: (630) 961-2168
www.sourcebooks.com

Holloway, Gillian.
  The complete dream book of love and relationships : discover what your dreams and intuition reveal about you and your love life / by Gillian Holloway.
      p. cm.
  Includes bibliographical references and index.
  1. Dream interpretation. 2. Love. 3. Man-woman relationships. 4. Interpersonal relations. I. Title.
  BF1091.H565 2010
  154.6'3--dc22

2009050700

Printed and bound in the United States of America.
VP 10 9 8 7 6 5 4 3 2 1

To everyone who dreams of love.

CONTENTS

ACKNOWLEDGMENTS

Thanks to Shana Drehs of Sourcebooks for her vision and expertise in igniting this project.

Thank you to the entire team at Sourcebooks: you are fabulous, fun, and ahead of the curve!

Special thanks to my publicist Eleanor Van Natta for her spirit and hard work!

Thanks to the women and men who generously shared their dreams, stories, and passions with me over the years. Your kindness, guts, spirit, and belief in passion have deepened my faith in life and love.

Thank you to my family, Pat, Doug, and Dev, for your support and humor.

Thank you to Rich for your kindness and encouragement.

Thanks, as always, to my dream buddies—Tracy, Peg, Kendra, and Norma Jean—for your ongoing brilliant sanity and huge, huge hearts.

Thank you to Larry for keeping the Lifetreks.com website research project on track and for generously offering technical wizardry during critical junctures.

Special thanks to Lea Sevey for teaching me so much about intuition over the years and remaining my go-to resource on the mysterious.

Introduction

How Dreams and Intuition Can Help You Discover and Deepen Love

It is difficult knowing who is right for you and who is wasting your time, who is trustworthy and who is unstable, unscrupulous, or even dangerous. We try to apply logic to the situation, and that helps. But most of us in the dating world find that we are perfectly capable of making terrible mistakes and of caring quite deeply about someone who has few redeeming features or who just isn't a good fit for us.

Friends can tell you what they believe about the situation and what they find is true for them; a therapist can tell you guidelines about relationships in general. Family members can tell you what they hope you will find in life.

What you need, though, is someone who knows your secrets, your emotional nature, your history of sabotage, your fear of intimacy, and your fear of winding up alone. You need someone who is absolutely and unreservedly on your side, who agrees that a solid, loving relationship is worth the quest.

In the pursuit of finding and nourishing love, you should take advantage of all the advocates, advisers, and supporters you can find, but the one resource you absolutely must take advantage of is your deeper mind. This part of your psyche takes in volumes of information, even subtle or subliminal clues; it recognizes patterns sometimes in an instant; and it knows and understands your personality without judgment and the ways your quirks and your strengths impact your style of relating and your approach to love.

The bottom line is that the deeper mind is one of your most accurate and potent advisers, and it tends to speak to you through your dreams and your intuition.

HOW DREAMS WORK

From the 1950s through the 1970s, a psychiatrist named Montague Ullman rocked the comfort zone of his colleagues by starting a worldwide movement that significantly changed the way people view their dreams. Known today as peer dreamwork, Ullman's technique is used to explore the feelings and potential meaning of a dream. Before the movement, dreams were considered diagnostic tools that therapists used to reveal what types of problems their patients might have. Ullman believed that, though dreams may be useful in that regard, they are far more than diagnostic tools.

In a nutshell, here are his three main concepts that opened the door to the modern exploration of how dreams work:

1. Dreams focus on the present in an attempt to make sense of current challenges, to preserve well-being, and to process information and stimulation. Dreams are simply the product of your mind constantly sorting through information and stimulation, and often presenting a distilled version of events in story form. Even when the past is woven into our dreams, it is because the deeper mind is trying to make sense of questions and goals we face in the present.

2. Dreams belong to the dreamer. Anyone who remembers and thoughtfully considers the meaning of a dream may perceive its implications and benefit from it. There is nothing inherently clinical or dangerous about attempting to discover the meaning in a dream.

3. Exploring dreams with friends or in a peer dream group can be an enriching process in which mutual support and exploration can benefit the entire group. Ullman encouraged people to form groups to share and discuss their dreams in a thoughtful, respectful style, so that individuals could explore their dreams among friends and peers, draw conclusions, and consider the implications for themselves.

Dream Vigilance: Your Threat Assessment

Ullman is also famous for a theory he called dream vigilance. He noticed that as many as three-quarters of the dreams people reported to him were unsettling or downright troubling. Yet the dreamers who were telling these dreams were not unstable and were not really in any objective trouble. He realized that the dreaming process tends to focus on threats to our happiness long before anything bad actually happens. A part of the mind is like a watchful sentinel in a tower, looking into the distance to see whether any enemies or threats appear on the horizon. When Ullman tracked the events associated with these dreams, he also found that the dreams exaggerated the potential for threat, amplified it, and put it into story form. If a dream predicted trouble, it was sometimes because change was happening and there was a potential for a problem—it was not that the trouble would necessarily come to pass.

Ullman's theory of dream vigilance has gone a long way to help us understand that dreams often have an edgy quality, even when things are going pretty well in our waking lives. This helps explain why our dreams can contain hypothetical scenarios in the future, often asking "What if...?" and playing out possibilities. Our dreams often recognize potential threats long before we do on a conscious level.

Romantic Dream Vigilance: Your Love Assessment

Your deeper mind not only is constantly scanning for threats but also is constantly searching for intensity or change of any kind. Your psyche registers the potential for happiness in your current situation and gauges the degree to which any individual you know might fit you as a romantic partner. The dreaming mind seems to have a bias toward relationships and community—toward being wholesomely connected with others and being fulfilled in love. Even when romance is not consciously on your mind, it remains a priority in your deeper mind. As a result, you will find yourself dreaming about it. Just as a part of your mind is always looking out for trouble, acting as an early warning system, a part of your mind is always scanning for romance and the potential for fulfilling partnership, acting as a kind of internal matchmaker.

A NOTE OF CAUTION

The dreaming mind is highly symbolic, and we should not take most of the elements in our dreams literally. Dreams tend to depict our life experiences in physical terms: something happens to our body, we are hurt, we bleed, we cough up food, we are pregnant, we try to find a toilet, or we discover a growth or parasite. People who remember dreams frequently are all too familiar with their graphic nature.

People who are less familiar with dreams may be shocked by the sometimes grisly or frightening images in some of the dreams discussed in this book. Perhaps because our interest in relationships is so central to our emotions and sense of fulfillment, dreams that tackle the issues associated with relationships and love are often shocking and even disturbing. When you see how the meaning of these dreams unfolds and offers help, I hope you will learn to appreciate the gift of this symbolic language. Startling dreams are normal, not unusual, so do not be alarmed or dismayed by some of the vivid dreams you will read.

THE RESEARCH FOR THIS BOOK

My own work with dreams began in the late 1980s, when I was working toward my doctorate in psychology. I began attending peer dream groups and discovered firsthand the excitement of sharing dreams and discovering individual insights that could benefit the entire group. In the 1990s, I began collecting dreams and the background stories of the individuals who shared them—the type of work they did; whether they felt stress; their age, gender, and spiritual orientation; and most important, what they felt was the meaning of their dreams. This collection of dreams and dreamer profiles has grown to more than thirty thousand, and the detailed profiles have enabled me to see how certain situations in life are associated with particular dream themes and imagery.

Dreams tend to have unique elements that are private and special to each dreamer. It is not possible to say unequivocally that a particular image always and only means one specific thing. Instead, for people to fully explore their associations to images and the feelings of their dreams, it is ideal for them to get together with others who are interested in dreams and share them in an unrushed and respectful fashion. With that said, however, we can take advantage of the research on modern symbolism and dream themes, and we can begin individual explorations of a dream by considering what similar dreams have suggested to others who observed the same theme or imagery.

For the past fifteen years, I have taught university courses on the psychology of intuition—the study of how we detect information, process it rapidly, and come up with answers that sometimes seem like magic. There are some theories that intuition is associated with our biological heritage, a kind of evolved survival instinct that can save our lives and help us make uncannily good decisions. There also seem to be styles of intuition, like personality traits, that enable some people to be lucky at love or shrewd in business. I've come to believe that everyone has intuition, which can be strengthened and amplified to our immense advantage when we routinely pay attention to it. If you love someone, your intuitive antenna is tuned to his station; you cannot help but pick up on his thoughts, his moods, and sometimes even his experiences.

When you are in danger or when you face an important crossroad in your life, your dreams open up a window to your intuitive nature. If you take advantage of this access that nature has made available, you will have a better chance of getting at the truth of a situation and of making the right decision.

There is no great trick to getting in sync with your intuitive nature. You just have to make it a practice to check in with your intuition and then get out of your own way. In this book, I will share with you the most effective suggestions I've found over the years for maximizing your intuition to gain clarity, to understand relationships, and to find love.

Follow the Instincts of the Happy Hearts

In my research about dreams that have come true and about intuitive flashes that have changed lives, an experience that comes up often is that of people finding and recognizing the person who was to be their mate. Those who have found the love of their life fascinate me. Like making a fortune, becoming famous, or winning an Olympic gold medal, these people beat the odds and live happily ever after. Although there does seem to be an element of serendipity involved in the stories of happy couples, there are some surprising common factors as well. People who find fulfilling partnerships and have happy marriages tend to behave in a certain way, to make certain types of decisions, and to have a certain perspective. They used not only common sense but also their gut instinct in choosing their partners, and they often had deliberately prepared for love in advance of meeting their partner. We'll look at the experiences of these couples throughout the book.

How This Book Works

You'll discover that it is human nature to be able to understand your dreams, to hear the voice of your intuition, and to make decisions that will help your relationships blossom and thrive, and this book will show you how to do all of that.

In chapter 1, we will look at a quality called brilliant sanity, a spontaneous flash of emotional intelligence and intuition that is talked about in Buddhist philosophy and in many works of psychology. You'll learn about your brilliant sanity, which bubbles up naturally, and how to make the most of it.

In chapter 2, you will learn about your romantic style and any tendencies you may have in relationships. We will review the types of dreams that each personality type is likely to have and the ways that your intuitive style can strengthen your awareness. Although you may have a mixture of the styles discussed here, you will learn how to avoid common pitfalls and feel more confident in your decisions about relationships.

In chapter 3, we will look at common beliefs and misconceptions about love that can cause us to miss love that is right in front of us. We'll talk about how your dreams make these misconceptions clear and how awareness of myths can free you to experience a more satisfying relationship.

Chapter 4 explores patterns in romantic relationships and ways your dreams and your gut instinct can highlight repeating patterns so that you are free to find and create the type of relationship you truly want.

Chapter 5 explores must-haves and deal breakers, the priorities and undesirable qualities that your dreams can make clearer.

In chapter 6 we'll explore dreams of the future and the possibility that your dreaming mind can give you hints of what's to come.

Chapter 7 reveals signs of love. We will look at what really happens when people meet the love of their life; the dreams, intuitions, and impressions that people report when they find real love; and the ways your intuition and your body can help you know what is true for you.

In chapter 8, we'll look at intuitive warning signs and warning dreams associated with problem relationships, poor choices, and threats on the horizon.

In chapter 9, you will read about common relationship dreams and what they can tell you about your personality and about the person you are seeing. This chapter also explores some of the most common symbols in relationship dreams and what they say about your real-life romance.

In chapter 10, you will learn how to program your dreams, setting the stage to find answers in your dreams and to better understand a relationship. We'll also explore the intuitive wisdom of the heart and the sensations of your body, maybe some of your best tools for knowing when someone is being truthful, when you have good rapport, and when a relationship has promise for the future.

**Some of the dreams and stories in the chapters that follow have been compressed and paraphrased for reasons of clarity. To protect privacy, some names and identifying characteristics of individuals have been changed.

Chapter 1

BRILLIANT SANITY, DREAMS, AND INTUITION

Your Ultimate Relationship Coach

Within you is a core of wisdom that Buddhist teachers call brilliant sanity. It is an intelligence that turns toward the truth the way a plant turns toward the sun: instinctively. This wisdom can operate with insufficient facts, accurately assessing the future and maintaining your sense of clarity even as you contend with situations fraught with emotion or desire. This wisdom tends not only to perceive reality clearly but also to view yourself and others with kindness and compassion. This doesn't mean you operate like a psychic sponge, taking on the problems of others out of concern—you can maintain strong, healthy boundaries and still have compassion for others. What it does mean is that your core of brilliant sanity tends to be kind, and part of that kindness is a loving understanding of yourself, of what you need, and of what your unique nature requires in order to feel fulfilled in a loving relationship.

You have already encountered this trait in yourself. Think about it: Do you sometimes sense who is calling when the phone rings, or know just where to look for a lost item even though someone else misplaced it? Can you sometimes find parking places by almost feeling their location? You may know just the right thing to say to people, to help them relax or start to open up. You may know what is really going on with others, in a way that they miss, when they experience a misunderstanding or a lack of communication. The best tool you have for navigating the landscape of love, for keeping yourself safe, for finding and nourishing the relationships you need, is this vital instinct, this deep intelligence that appears with flashes of brilliance: brilliant sanity.

Intuitive signals and dreams are two ways that your deeper core of wisdom communicates and expresses itself. There is nothing spooky about this; it is a natural part of your intelligence reflecting aspects of your experience that may not yet be at the forefront of your awareness. In some cases, dreams and intuition appear to be almost magic because, through them, we become aware of information or insights that have been obscured or hidden. At any given time, you know more than you can be aware of consciously, and your flashes of insight and your dreams demonstrate this deeper knowing; they not only reflect what is going on in your life but also highlight what is most important to understand in your relationships.

If you are like many of the women in my classes, you are frustrated because you have excellent instincts about other people's relationships, and feel a little blind or confused about your own. Why is it that we can be so brilliant and intuitive about some parts of life, yet feel bewildered and cut off from our own wisdom in other parts of life?

THE THREE BLINDERS: IMPORTANCE, DESIRE, AND FEAR

When a situation is extremely important to us, we have a tendency to go blank on our instincts and to overthink the situation.

When there is a powerful emotional component, and when there is something in the situation that we fear as well as something we desire, these things can clog our ability to hear our inner wisdom or understand our gut instincts. That is why when you are talking with friends about their situations you may have excellent instincts and a feeling that you know what is going on and how it will play out. But when you are trying to get a sense of clarity with a romance of your own, you may be inadvertently blocking your core knowing because of fear, desire, and a personal investment in the outcome.

When we deal with romance, sometimes wishful thinking, small resentments, desperation and loneliness, or even a false feeling of worthlessness easily confuse us. This may ignite an urge to try to fool someone into loving us, or cause us to feel like an imposter. Both men and women feel the stakes are high, our feelings are hooked, and it is easy to feel we must captivate and conceal our "flaws" in order to be loved. Of course, these thoughts are illusions, but when we deal with fear and desire, we tend to drift away from that core of brilliant sanity and forget not only what we really want but also who we really are. When we abandon the core self, for whatever reason, we also detach from our intuition and our truth-detector.

If you have been hurt by love (and who hasn't?), you may search for a partner, but all the while be tracing your scars and probing old wounds. When you meet new people, the matchmaker in your heart may feel a flutter of hope while the district attorney in your mind is ready to indict them for crimes they could never have committed. I know people who strap on their bitterness when they go out to meet someone new, like a western gunslinger buckling his gun belt, and then wait, hand poised over their weapon, for a person to make one false move so they can gun him down. It is understandable that even the most resilient among us is wary and bruised, and that in the search for companionship we alternate between romantic fantasies and flinty-eyed cynicism.

Despite these tendencies to approach the topic of love with divided concerns, your instinct for happiness is still intact, and your ability to know what is real and to do the right thing for yourself is alive and well. The brilliance at your core is always speaking to you through your dreams and your subtle intuitions. If you slow down and listen, you will often find that you already know what is true about a situation and that you already know how you really feel about someone.

Flashes of Knowing

Rachel met a man at a party and instantly identified him as the person who had been stalking her with obscene phone calls. She had shaken his hand because he was a friend of a friend, and in a second, it flashed through her mind that he was the one. Another woman, Rebecca, saw the shoulder of a man she did not know at a party and knew in a second that this was the man she would marry. These flashes of knowing arise from our intuition; our brilliant sanity recognizes them as things that are crucial for us to know.

Everyone has this capacity, and one of the best ways to have it function well in our lives is to discuss it and pay attention to it. Flashes of knowing also are the part of you that lets you know when you need to slow down, take a breath, and get back to your center if you have been racing at high speed for too long. In relationships, this coming back to your center is critical for understanding another person and for making decisions with confidence.

Research into intuition suggests that our first impressions are quite often accurate, yet many of us have a difficult time accepting the wave of knowing that rises from within. I've talked to some folks who have experienced miserable marriages, and they have told me that they knew as they walked down the aisle that they were making a terrible mistake. They argued with themselves that the sense of dread they felt was simply a case of cold feet, not to be taken seriously. They told themselves they had to be mature, to make a commitment, to keep a bargain they didn't really want, when some knowledge of the heart said, "Don't."

THE TABOO OF THE SUBJECTIVE

For whatever reason, it almost seems as if we were brainwashed to discount our core of instincts, intuition, and brilliant sanity. Perhaps in our love affair with technology and science, our worship of facts and discoveries, we have become doubtful of information that presents itself through subjective awareness. Whatever the reason, it takes boldness to listen to your personal wisdom, to give it credence, to follow the warning in your gut or attend to the thought that flashes across your mind.

Many of us, myself included, try to argue with our feelings of fear, almost scolding ourselves if we feel doubtful about someone or if we feel reluctant to place ourselves at risk. It seems at times that we feel we are breaking an unspoken rule if we choose to listen to what we know and honor what is true for us. Those of us who choose to become better acquainted with the brilliance that lives inside of us must be ready to break through the taboo that we shouldn't listen to what our intuition is telling us.

THE MYTH OF REASONABLENESS

Cathy's Story

Years ago, a client of mine took a temporary job that placed her in the company of a man she had once been engaged to marry. Ryan was powerful, attractive, sensual, and obsessive. Cathy had broken off their engagement when Ryan's behavior had become suffocating and exhausting. He had not exactly stalked her afterward, but he had made it clear that he was not giving up on her. She had stayed clear of him for a year and felt safe that that chapter of her life was behind her and that they had both moved on. When her boss placed her on assignment in Ryan's company, Cathy had the option of refusing the placement, but she didn't really think that was necessary, even though she had a dragging feeling in the pit of her stomach. Whenever doubts occurred, she would argue with herself in a bracing way and insist to herself that they would merely have a professional relationship.

Yet it was soon apparent that the chemistry between them was far from gone. Whenever they were together, there was a charge in the room like ozone in the air before a lightning storm. Cathy noticed people glancing back and forth between them, assessing the drama beneath the surface. At that point, she began to experience a division in herself. (When you feel divided, split down the middle, or awash with feelings that don't match your thoughts, it can be a sign that brilliant sanity is battling with the prerecorded message to be reasonable.)

Cathy felt depressed and tired, physically dragged down, and she was having difficulty concentrating. But she was also feeling flattered by Ryan's attentions. He was the dominant male in their work environment, the big boss, and he was attractive and dynamic. She felt feminine and desirable under the hot spotlight of his attraction. Cathy spent more time talking with herself, arguing with some deeper awareness, and insisting that it was a manageable situation. Because she was arguing with her own core of wisdom, she began to feel confused. Perhaps, she wondered, she had made a mistake to break off their engagement—after all, Ryan clearly still passionately cared for her after all this time. It was also clear that many women at the company found him extremely attractive and would have loved to be the object of his attention. Whenever she tried to reason out the situation, instead of arriving at a logical conclusion, her thoughts took her in a circle, like an amusement park ride, and left her disoriented and fatigued.

But the brilliant sanity inside us is never extinguished, no matter how we refute it or confuse ourselves. It crops up in feelings, thoughts, coincidences, and dreams. In the midst of her situation, Cathy began to have startling nightmares. In one dream, some thugs held her hostage and forced her to build a box of some kind. With growing horror, she realized that she was actually building a coffin, and that it was her own coffin! When she completed the task, the men dragged her outside, gave her a shovel, and ordered her to dig. Shaking with fear, she realized she was digging her own grave. At that point, she woke up with a start.

Let's consider this dream together. It is easy to see that something is wrong. Cathy felt that the dream might have had to do with her dislike of her work because it was boring and didn't provide her with an opportunity to grow. But instinctively, as we explored it, both Cathy and I sensed that the drama of her dream was so intense that this explanation didn't account for the horror presented. Building your own coffin is a step-by-step process, as is digging your own grave: both images hint at a progressive movement toward a grim result. In addition, the larger plot of being held captive by thugs seems to suggest an overall lack of freedom or being controlled by others.

When Cathy and I discussed the sense of feeling controlled and being a captive, she inevitably thought of the situation with Ryan, partly because he had been very controlling in their former relationship, and partly because her present situation affected her in so many different ways that she was essentially paralyzed by it. Each day she spent working there made her feel less like herself and more mesmerized and confused.

Was Ryan ultimately planning to murder her? Well, that is certainly possible, but she did not feel that that was likely or that such a warning was the essential meaning of her dream. She did feel, however, that the dream was showing her the evolution of her current strategy of reasonableness and going with the flow, against what she knew deep down to be true for her: this man, their chemistry, and the situation at his company were not good for her.

Unlike our tendency to complicate situations, dreams try to simplify them for us. Certain things and people in life make us feel more alive and nourish us, the way sunshine, water, and fresh air nourish plants. Other things and people make us feel less alive, drain our vitality, destroy our confidence, and muddle our mind. The wisdom at your core is basic: it warns you of situations that are poisonous to your vitality, to your spark, by essentially saying, "That road leads to being less alive!"

No More Crazy Love

Cathy lost no time extricating herself from her assignment, and she made it clear to Ryan that the past was long over. Surprisingly, after a brief flurry of attempts to contact her, he gave up and left her alone. She also learned something about her inner wisdom that has altered the way she approaches romantic relationships in general. Cathy has a compass inside that points toward what makes her happy, what gives her energy, what restores her faith and joy in life. She has never again engaged in what she calls crazy love, that enticing alchemy of sexual energy that comes with unhealthy strings attached. She trusts her dreams and her instincts to warn her of missteps early on, and although she is not sure if she ultimately wishes to marry or not, she has rewarding, genuinely loving relationships that are fulfilling and passionate, that don't hold her back or make her feel small. Perhaps most important, Cathy feels connected with her ability to know what is true for her and to make choices based on that awareness. She feels connected with her core of wisdom, and she trusts herself.

EMBRACE YOUR BRILLIANCE AND BREAK THE TABOO: TRUST YOURSELF

Trusting yourself is a process. You have learned over time that you can do certain things well without much effort. You know how to guess right within certain frameworks, with people, with money, at work, or in your hobbies. You have evidence of your brilliance in some contexts and have no trouble trusting your instincts and your ability to improvise and problem solve in those settings. Part of the reason you trust yourself is that you've accumulated evidence in the form of past successes. It's clear that you know what you're doing, so you can relax, do what you do best, be present in the moment, and trust your own reactions.

Another reason you trust yourself is that you have acquired a habitual posture of emotional and psychological balance in those areas where experience has shown that you "just know" how to make the right decisions. You don't engage in circular thinking or worry that you might be wrong when you need to make decisions quickly. Even when there is stress involved, you know how to keep your balance the way a downhill skier crouches for speed or the way a surfer rides a wave. You find yourself doing the right thing even before you have entirely thought it through sometimes, because your emotional balance lets you naturally perform at a high level and lets your brilliant sanity emerge unimpaired. You probably know when someone simply wants to waste your time in the workplace, and you probably have a strong sense of when a project is a good one or when a product will be a profitable one to add to your lineup.

Without really knowing it, many of us give ourselves permission to be brilliant and clear in certain areas, but we deny ourselves permission to fully access our instincts in other areas. This functions a little bit like the permissions set on our computers: when we want to know answers in areas where we don't have permission to be wise, we get an error message in the form of self-doubt, self-criticism, or reminders to be reasonable or not to be silly. Internal static is not a sign that you lack wisdom, but it can be a sign that you have not given yourself permission to access or trust your wisdom.

Pause now and consider where you trust yourself, where you keep your balance effortlessly, and where you have permission to access your inner wisdom. You may want to have a piece of paper ready so that you can jot down answers to the following questions.

In what areas of life do you feel you have good instincts? What kind of evidence, in the form of past experiences, do you remember about those areas? Think of times when you might not have had access to necessary information, but nevertheless you knew what to do somehow. Most of us don't count the almost-daily experiences at the office when we have to complete a project without the data we would have liked to have on hand. Since we have to finish, we just do the project anyway.

In what situations of your life do you find that you somehow keep your emotional and psychological balance despite objective stress? Are you calm in the center of the storm at work? Do you translate conversations for people who can't seem to understand one another? Do you read your loved ones like a book, and sense what they need to feel better when they're down? These may be situations in which other people say, "How do you do that? I'd be a nervous wreck." I know a woman who brings calm and healing to others by volunteering as a victim's advocate when there has been a suicide or a violent death. She is one of the first people to arrive on the scene to be there to hold the weeping family members. Most of us would want to be helpful but would find the situation overwhelming or too sad. This woman, though, becomes clearer in this setting and finds it easy to know what to say and do to offer comfort and calm. She exhibits brilliant sanity in the midst of tragedy.

Where do you have permission to use your instincts? Is it okay to have good instincts for others but not for yourself? Is it okay to do well at your job but not at your personal life? Do you have permission to try hard but not to succeed? Do you have permission to understand love, or are you supposed to get confused? You may not have a strong sense of the answers to these questions yet; if that is the case, then just make notes about what you suspect may be true for you.

Romantic love is a context in which we often do not give ourselves permission to trust what we know. We do not feel that we have sufficient evidence of our brilliance, and we have trouble keeping emotional and psychological balance. For these reasons, even the most intuitive and wise among us can feel blocked and confused as we try to navigate the waters of love.

Fortunately, even though we are each unique, we can learn very rapidly from the successes and observations of others. We can learn the language of inner wisdom through the stories of others, and this triggers greater awareness of how our own sense of certainty can become stronger, leading us away from disappointment and toward love.

How Your Dreams and Intuition Assess Relationships

Have you noticed that sometimes friends know before you do when something is off about a new person in your life, or when someone would be good for you? Of course, this could be because your friends understand your temperament and what makes you happy. But it's also because friends are not attached to any particular fantasy about someone you've met. They are neutral, wanting only your happiness.

This is exactly the way your deeper mind operates, too. This part of yourself is aware of the importance of love and relationships and wants you to be happy, whatever form that takes. This part of you is not swept away by a handsome face or an exciting story told over dinner. It is not impressed by money, glibness, false attentiveness, or other methods of seduction. Genuine caring, consistency, and warmth impress your deeper mind. It is the ultimate lie detector, and if you tune into it, you will be able to spot a phony quickly, no matter how smooth that phony's presentation might be. You will also sense when to give someone time and allow a friendship or relationship to unfold. Some of the finest people you will meet will not give razzle-dazzle first impressions but will have the depth to be interested in your story and your needs. The following sections go over some ways that your intuitive knowing may find expression.

Romantic Memory Imprints

Whenever you care about someone, regardless of how the relationship ends, that person becomes an imprint in your memory. Later, if you date someone who has similar behavioral patterns, your deeper mind will recognize the similarity—even if the two look nothing alike or have different personalities and interests. You will likely dream that you are back in a relationship with the person from your past, much to your surprise. Or you may find that past love flashing through your mind, seemingly for no reason. When you are with the new person, the relationship from your past may flicker through your memory. Pay attention to these cues, because they mean that your deeper mind is recognizing similarities and is trying to bring this awareness to your consciousness.

Sandy's Story

Sandy is a lovely woman who was married and had a child with a very handsome, wealthy, intriguing man. He was worldly and came with all the accessories that Hollywood encourages us to admire. At the time of their marriage, she was a model and he was a very successful businessman. After the birth of their child, though, Sandy's priorities changed; she no longer wished to model and chose to stay home with their daughter. In very short order, her husband changed from the glossy hunk she had married to a snarling critic who treated her like she had committed a crime by getting pregnant, having their child, and wanting to enjoy motherhood. Although at first she couldn't believe it, she came to realize that he didn't want a family—he had wanted a stunning model to complete his image and to be his hot playmate. He felt that she had betrayed him by wanting a family and making their child a priority.

He scolded her because her figure was not bikini perfect after the baby, and he seemed uninterested in their child. After a short stage of bewilderment, she realized that, emotionally, her husband was no husband at all. He didn't want or understand the real woman she was, and worst of all, he did not want their beautiful baby. When she asked him whether he wanted a divorce, he leaped at the suggestion, and they parted quickly. He went on to another gorgeous woman, and Sandy went back to her hometown to raise her daughter and find a way to make a living.

Years passed, and she became very successful in real estate. Sandy remained single for many years while her daughter grew into a lovely girl. Sandy had no trouble finding men who were interested in relationships with her, because she was always a gorgeous woman and had lots of spirit and an engaging personality. However, Sandy often found that she was really interested only in men who were larger than life, extremely eligible, and successful, with numerous homes around the world and a high lifestyle. She often had affairs with these jet-set guys, although the relationships tended to end badly and abruptly. She asked me why she so often dreamed that she was back in her marriage, being criticized and cast aside for being herself. She assured me that she would never go back to her husband for any reason in the world. His coldness toward their daughter had changed her feelings toward him forever.

We talked about the concept of the psychological imprint:

how the mind uses an early experience in life as a shorthand memory that describes an entire pattern of behavior and emotional relating. I asked her whether it was possible that she was dreaming of her marriage, not because of unfinished business with her ex-husband, but because of current business with similar types of men, ones who desired her but did not really care about her, men who had a great deal to offer in terms of lifestyle but little or nothing to offer in terms of heart. She felt strongly that her deeper mind was indeed showing her that she was in similar types of relationships, with similar drawbacks and explosive endings.

This is an example of how the conscious mind has its agenda and priorities while the deeper mind has a clearer sense of where our happiness lies. Many times, we may miss cues or repeat the same wrong turn on life's path by ignoring our deeper mind.

Sandy gave a great deal of thought to her dreams and her intuition. It dawned on her that focusing on Mercedes-Benz cars and vacation homes in warm climates was not the way to find a generous-hearted lover who could really understand her and help her create a home.

She attended a friend's large wedding and ran into her most recent lover there. He ogled her in her low-cut dress and remarked caustically that she was nearly bursting out of it. She moved quickly away from him and encountered a kind-looking man whom she barely knew standing nearby. She quickly engaged him in conversation and soon found herself appreciating the way he looked into her eyes rather than at her bosom while they talked. Furthermore, although he was not conventionally handsome, the laugh lines around his eyes softened his rugged face. She liked the warmth of his gaze and the respectful way he spoke to her. She knew something about him from mutual friends. He was a home builder who was stable and successful, though not wealthy. They soon started dating, and she told me that she couldn't get over how nice he was. He did things to help her and her daughter; he learned to ride horses, which were a passion of hers; and he was obviously devoted to her. After a year or so, they married, and today they are still happily devoted, several years later.

Sandy's happiness was there for her once she stopped being dazzled by the superficial trappings of success and power that had once seemed so attractive to her. Obviously, there is nothing wrong with admiring achievement, and the moral of this story is not that wealthy men cannot also be good men. But in this case, Sandy was obscuring the wisdom of her deeper mind by continuing to chase the things that had nothing to do with her genuine happiness. Once she stopped jamming the channel of her own intuition, she was led to the love of her life in very short order. When she saw that she was really having the same relationship over and over with different men, she became free to recognize and experience the joy of a man who listened to her; who found her personality adorable; who loved kids and pets; and who wanted to be with her, not merely possess her.

Flashback Dreams

Pay attention to your dreams when you have just met someone new or have just started dating someone. You will likely have dreams that refer to past partners or past experiences. If those flashback dreams are about relationships that you would not want to repeat, pay attention. There may be good reason to reconsider or to proceed with caution in the relationship, or at the very least to monitor yourself to see if you are slipping into an old pattern that you have already found unfulfilling in the past. If the dreams are about relationships that were happy while they lasted, your deeper mind may be recognizing a quality that is nourishing to you in a partner.

Symbolic Shorthand Dreams

In your dreams, is the new person you've met nice to you or cruel? Does he focus on you or on himself? Do you find yourself asking questions in your dreams about whether or not this person could really be right for you? Surprisingly, your dreams can be months ahead of you in noticing things that don't work for you or will take time for you to work out and understand. Look at the bottom line of these dreams—typically there is an intuitive thumbs-up or thumbs-down signal.

For example, Jade had a date with a new fellow, and afterward had a dream that her gums were bleeding. In waking life, of course, bleeding gums are a definite signal that something is wrong, although the problem is the sort of thing that you might overlook or not take seriously at first. As it happened, this new fellow had problems that were fairly serious but didn't jump out immediately. Because of her dream, Jade was more alert to potential trouble and saw more clearly some things that she didn't want to take on in a romantic relationship.

Tina dated a man for a while, and although he kept telling her he was crazy about her, he also was rather critical of her in a way that she didn't like but that always seemed reasonable or logical to her in the context. He corrected her grammar when she was trying to tell a story and would joke about her progress in her career as if it were amusing that she was actually succeeding. Then Tina had a dream that she came out to start her car one morning and all four tires were flat: entirely deflated. This dream helped her to have more confidence in the truth that this man was shaking her confidence in herself at a time when she was succeeding in life in a way that she had not done before.

Tina realized that she was beginning to feel a loss of her normal buoyancy and confidence because of the man's way of interacting with her and because of the way she took his criticism to heart. She didn't dump him simply because of the dream, but she did feel better about trusting her subjective awareness of what was going on. When they hit a rocky patch, she felt confident in letting the connection go without regret. She immediately felt more like herself again, another sign that a relationship is not nourishing.

Although you may not want to base your entire assessment of a potential new partner on a dream, do take signs like these into account, and be awake, armed with your intuition as things unfold. Even if you can't bring yourself to believe what your dreams tell you, you will be able to react faster if you need to. You'll be much less surprised or hurt if someone lets you down, and you'll feel more confidence in your ability to trust yourself by paying attention to the implications of your dreams.

Peculiar Patterns

A peculiar pattern—even a small one—that repeats in a relationship may be a subtle signal of something important. Pay attention to patterns that seem out of place, unusual, or troubling, even if you cannot explain why they make you uncomfortable.

Kristin launched into a fun and fabulous affair with an unusual man she really liked. They had a humorous rapport and a lot of fun together. Although he was a fairly athletic guy, and they were both young, she noticed that he was awfully clumsy, and that surprised her. Specifically, he seemed to slip often and accidentally bump her or step on her foot. When she got in and out of the car, when she was carrying something, or when they went through a doorway, he often seemed to misjudge the distance and would bump into her or even accidentally hit her. He always apologized lovingly, saying, "Oh, sorry, honey, I'm so clumsy." Something about this bothered her, but she couldn't put her finger on it.

The mere sensation that something is wrong is often a signal from the deeper mind that you should take seriously. Your bodily sensations can be like the language of your dreams, arising from a deeper wisdom and illustrating important truths about your situation and your feelings. One day, they got into a heated argument, and the man struck Kristin so hard in the face that the blow lifted her off the ground. As she lay face down on the floor, her ears ringing, the many times this man had "accidentally" hit her flashed through her mind. "It was there all the time," she told me later. "He was repeatedly unconsciously hitting me, and I didn't see that as a part of him; I saw it as an accident. But in a way, it was like his subconscious mind was telling mine: I like to hit women." If this pattern had been part of a dream, Kristin might have recognized that it potentially held important meaning for her. In a similar way, we can sometimes interpret as meaningful a repetitive situation that comes with a peculiar feeling in the body if we pause to consider it and allow ourselves to fully explore the sensation without labeling it or dismissing it in a hurry.

The Instinctive Friendship Feeling

The next time you meet someone new, instead of evaluating career success, body, or last name, evaluate the friendship factor first. Is this someone you could be friendly with even if a romantic relationship did not blossom? Could you tell this person private things about yourself, or did you feel you had to put on your game face? If you answered no to the first question, this doesn't mean you can't have the sparks and the wow factor as well; but happy couples are friends, and they seem to realize this almost instantly.

We may fantasize about falling into bed with someone, but just as often, the initial meeting of happily married couples resulted in their staying up all night talking, like best friends who had been apart for years and had a lot of catching up to do. We aren't taught to fantasize about meeting someone terrific and having the conversation of a lifetime, but maybe we should be. These folks tell me that when they went home finally, they knew that the other person was going to be someone very important because of a feeling they have only when they are with very close and old friends.

The subjective feeling of friendship is accurate: even though you might not have known the other person for long, you have an instinctive feeling of trust—you can obviously communicate with each other, and there is a joy in pouring out observations, anecdotes, and experiences. You are trying not to impress the other person but to share.

THE IMPLICATIONS OF ENLISTING YOUR INTUITION

I don't mean to imply that you should throw out logic or disregard the attributes you find appealing in a potential partner. But I hear many stories, such as the ones you've read about in this chapter, from women who have been astounded to find that when they stopped looking for what they thought they wanted, they suddenly found what really makes them happy. What they discovered is that intuition and brilliant sanity offer greater awareness of what is really going on with a potential partner and of how that person could impact you in the future.

Sometimes people worry that if they pay attention to their dreams and their intuition, they will learn things they would rather not know and will have to make decisions they would rather not make. This dread of inner truth is counterproductive and unnecessary. You are free to make any choices you like and to add up all the different elements involved to determine what you feel and what you want.

It is to your advantage, however, to consciously add your intuitive feelings into the mix as you make decisions. Your brilliant sanity and your intuition will minimize the damage of a disappointing experience and let you bounce back and into the arms of real love that much faster. Your deeper awareness will also help to give you a heads-up if you find yourself in one of those relationships where everything looks right and everything feels wrong. Learn to trust your gut and listen to the quiet voice inside that has no agenda except your happiness. This isn't a matter of making wild decisions on a whim—it is a matter of paying attention to what a part of you already knows and benefiting from that knowledge.

CLEAR YOUR INTUITIVE RADAR

Sometimes students and clients will tell me that their intuition does not work. They say they have absolutely no intuition at all or that it sometimes points them in the wrong direction. I believe that intuition is innate, associated with our survival instincts and a rapid-fire ability to recognize patterns with only minimal cues. This ability is always with us, and it does not get broken. However, like any kind of information-processing system, it can be clogged or blurred, and emotion and worry can overwhelm the ability to interpret subtle awareness.

I offer a statement to clients who feel they are out of sync with their intuition. You can read it aloud once a day to clear away the sense of being separated from your ability to discern clearly. Feel free to alter the wording to suit your style or your personal faith.

CLEARING STATEMENT

I accept the power and the clarity of my intuitive abilities. These are natural abilities that are a normal part of life and are not extraordinary or too much to hope for. I forgive any misunderstandings in my past related to the idea of intuition and embrace this potential in myself. All creatures in nature have a kind of intuition and instinct, and I am a part of nature. Whether or not I have been aware of it, I possess an unerring instinct for life. I accept my instinct for survival and my intuition for happiness. I know when something or someone is good for me and is life affirming, and I know when something is not right for me, too. I am building my relationship with this inner brilliance on a daily basis, understanding the signals and the voice of my intuition. By understanding how this feels and what it is like, I will be able to recognize my intuition before there is an urgent matter and emotions run high. I clear away any misperceptions, any illusions, and any false ideas now. I see clearly, I feel clearly, and I listen to my inner wisdom. I am free to make wise choices and to weigh my perceptions as I see fit. I am free. I am wise. I am whole. The truth empowers me and hurts no one.

Chapter 2

YOUR ROMANTIC PERSONALITY STYLE

Some people have found love by working from the inside out. They seem to understand what excites them, restores their spirit, and renews their energy. They know what they admire, respect, and need in a partner. These fortunate folks are not only clear thinkers; they are clear feelers, too, in the emotional sense. They don't fool themselves or feel conflicted about choices in relationships. Others, who know themselves less well, tend to get into relationship loops where they attract and move through very similar romantic patterns without even recognizing it. If you can begin a relationship from a place of self-awareness and clarity, you may find that choices will come easier for you. The first step is to identify your romantic style.

WHAT IS YOUR ROMANTIC STYLE?

In helping people decipher their relationship dreams, I have observed that women often approach romantic relationships in a particular style—one that stems from their personality and emotional needs. Relationships tend to run aground when core needs are not met or when priorities are not shared, or at least respected.

Often women do not discuss these core needs and personal styles with their partners because the women themselves are not aware of their priorities until something interferes with them or until they feel less alive in a relationship.

There is nothing rigidly scientific about the four relationship styles I will describe in the next few pages; they are based on clusters of personality traits that present themselves in dreams, in behaviors, and in the factors that enliven or extinguish our ability to relate.

The differences in these romantic styles can sometimes explain why one person's delight is another person's poison. Our priorities do change somewhat as we move through life, and many people feel that they are a blend of these styles. As you read the descriptions that follow, you may recognize your own romantic style, as well as find some pieces of the puzzle that help you understand what you need and why some objectively good partners were ultimately intolerable.

STYLE #1: THE SPARKLER

The Sparkler personality type is happiest with people around and is generally a gifted communicator. Sparklers can read people instantly and can move around a party or meeting like a hummingbird, exchanging with others on a fairly intimate level very quickly. Envious strangers might believe Sparklers are superficial, but in fact, Sparklers have the gift of creating instant rapport, fast intimacy, and rapid-growing relationships. Often this personality type is very attractive or has a quality of beauty, style, or charisma that is almost magnetic. Sparklers enjoy fashion, decor, and beautiful surroundings, and they are often cultured and well traveled.

Sparklers love variety, movement, and nice things, but not out of narcissism; rather, the Sparkler loves everything in life that is intriguing, beautiful, enriching, or exotic. Whether it is a gourmet recipe, a meditation process, or an art exhibit, the Sparkler wants to experience it. Sparklers can drink in beauty and variety and be completely renewed by them. A Sparkler is an excellent conversationalist, a lively companion, and can find the fun in almost any situation. Sparklers are warm friends and can be extremely caring and loyal, dipping into their formidable store of energy to help others.

A Sparkler has lots of charm, is typically high energy, and may be very attractive or exude sexual vibes that shout, "Hot stuff!" Conversation and variety actually give her energy and soothe her. After a stressful workweek, going to a party and making new and interesting friends will restore the Sparkler.

Sparklers' challenges in relationships are distinguishing among their many would-be partners and knowing themselves well enough to communicate their core needs clearly to those they attract. Because Sparklers derive energy from new acquaintances and shine brightly in the admiration of others, they can easily mistake the high of admiration and novelty for the joy of blossoming love.

A Sparkler's Relationship Loop

A Sparkler is a beautiful and charming person who easily captivates men and who enjoys the chase, the seduction, and the excitement of new relationships. Men seem to be easily smitten by her, understandably, and her typical relationship goes like this:

· There is rapid seduction, hot chemistry, and quick commitment to exclusivity, with discussions of marriage or a permanent partnership entering the conversation early on.

- She feels excited celebration, showing off of the new conquest for family review. There are lots of "This is it!" statements and behaviors on both sides. They review logistics—such as where to live and how it all will work—while still in the early days of the relationship.
- She being an ongoing recitation of the man's good qualities and special features, to herself, to her friends, and to her therapist.
- They settle into some kind of routine with extended visits at each person's home.
- They begin to have a realization of their differences: He wants quiet, and she wants people and parties. He wants all her attention, while she needs variety, freedom, and lots of new experiences.
- He cracks down, insisting that, if she loves him, she will shine only for him. She thinks this sounds reasonable and tries. She grows thin, pale, and cranky.
- She then experiences the rapid onset of stress symptoms: tension headaches, indigestion, cramps, allergy flare-ups, asthma symptoms, backaches, fatigue, and intermittent depression.
- She enters a period of fogginess, confusion, increased health flare-ups, anxiety dreams—she does not feel like herself. She loses interest in sex, which was their best subject together. He is hurt and bewildered. They fight.
- She picks fights with him, aggressively finding fault and making it difficult for him to hang on. At this point, she is trying to nudge the relationship to an end-point crisis and may or may not be consciously aware of it.
- They break up! She is very gracious about the whole thing and hopes that someday she will meet someone who is right. She resumes her normal activities and soon regains her normal sunny disposition and zest for life.

This is one relatively classic relationship loop for the Sparkler. If you are not a Sparkler, it is easy to assume these folks are shallow, narcissistic, or addicted to the spotlight. Although some "beautiful people" appear not to have developed in some ways, the sparkling personality is simply one that shines brightly and has an instinct for rapport. These people are restored by social interaction and by variety and stimulation. They literally feel sick and drained if they cannot have sufficient interaction. It is easy to assume that Sparklers are dabblers, because they sample so many different things. However, they are more than capable of sticking with some things, as long as they are free to investigate lots of new things on a regular basis. They make excellent journalists, event planners, publicists, talk-show hosts, teachers, facilitators, and sales representatives. I meet Sparklers often in my work in the psychology field, as they love to take new classes and are serious about their personal and spiritual growth.

A Sparkler's Dreams

Sparklers attract and are drawn to others quite easily, so they often dream of the attraction phase of a relationship. They dream of getting new cars, picking out delightful puppies, and moving into an ideal home when they are trying to evaluate a new romantic interest. Typically, these dreams reflect details of the good features of the new potential candidate (symbolized as the car, pet, or home). Because this personality type has few inhibitions to romance or intimacy, there are often few negatives apparent in their early dreams, when the relationship has not yet begun.

After a first date (or a contact sufficient for the deeper mind to start making connections), a Sparkler's dreams may change strikingly if there are qualities present in the other person that merit rapid attention and consideration. At this point, the Sparkler may have flashback dreams of being in a past relationship that was hurtful or confining. She may dream of trying to have sex with the other person but something unpleasant or unexpected ruins the moment. These dreams hint that there is some factor beneath the surface, either in the other person or in their chemistry as a couple, that makes the potential for intimacy more complex.

Lynn dreamed of a first kiss with a new man in which he put his tongue in her mouth, and she discovered it was forked, like a snake's. She did not find this sensual at all but alarming and weird. In waking life, she associated the term *forked tongue* with lying. She discovered through a mutual acquaintance that indeed he had not been truthful with her about some things in his background. For her, this disqualified him. She felt that if he would lie about small things, he might also be untruthful about larger, more important matters.

Yasmine dreamed of getting into a shiny speedboat with her new guy and zipping out into the sea. Away from shore, however, the engine broke down and they drifted in waters that were suddenly filled with shark fins. This ominous scene frightened her, and to some extent, it did foreshadow the course of their brief romance. After a speedy launch into their relationship, they didn't know how to be together, and their ability to communicate broke down (the drifting). They also fought a great deal because he had a style of verbal attack that he thought nothing of but that made her feel put down and devalued (being surrounded on all sides by sharks that might attack whenever she moved).

Sparkler personalities tend to have a lot of cautionary dreams because they are so turned on by new friendships, new possibilities, and new tingles of romance that they focus on the possibilities and make rapid-fire connections. The dreaming mind tends to point out the pitfalls of attractive strangers and fast-burning passion that can be mistaken for fulfilling partnership.

When a Sparkler does find a fulfilling partner, she may dream of returning to her hometown and finding absolute peace there for the first time. One woman met a man she felt content with and dreamed of being in love with her brother. This sounds disturbing, but the tone of the dream was happy, simple, and positive. It had nothing to do with incest, and she was not secretly attracted to her own brother. Instead, the dream highlighted qualities that her new friend had in common with her brother, who loved her unselfishly and with whom she had always felt that she could be herself. It was her deeper mind's way of suggesting that she had found a partner whose traits she already knew, loved, and trusted. She was with someone of her own tribe, so to speak, and the connection would be a deep one. Unlike her other relationships, this one has lasted and flourished.

A Sparkler's Intuition

Sparklers have strong intuitive signals and do well to pay attention to them. Their intuitive signals come typically in two forms: mental flashes and physical sensations or symptoms. They get flashes of understanding and images in their mind's eye, as if from nowhere. Inside their thoughts, there is an interruption and a flash of a scene or awareness, like a clip from a movie. They may also have strong gut feelings occasionally, but it is more typical for them to experience a sense of knowing in the mind.

Their brilliant sanity may guide them to make snap decisions, which to the casual observer may appear to be independent of known facts or objective data. They simply make a decision and watch themselves execute changes. When asked, they may not even be able to tell you how they knew to take a certain course of action; they just did. Typically, they have a terrific track record with real-world decisions in business or with property, money, and possessions.

When they are in a prolonged situation that's not right for them, Sparklers experience a dramatic drop in their personal energy. Usually they are the life of the party with boundless energy, but when they are going against their nature, they will feel chronically drained and muddled, a state completely unlike their normal disposition. This is when you will hear them say they don't feel like themselves.

When they get seriously off course, a variety of nasty and seemingly unrelated health problems can plague Sparklers. These can include indigestion with no known cause, menstrual complications that doctors cannot resolve, mysterious muscle aches and spasms, and sensitivities to foods or substances that do not register as allergens when tested. When this occurs, it is vital that Sparklers tune into themselves again and get back in touch with their own needs at the same time they seek medical attention and psycho-emotional support as needed. Sparklers need to consider whether their sense of energy drain is associated with the life choices they have been making. That is not to say that their health challenges are not real—they are—but they may coincide with a decision (or relationship) that pulls them away from their natural spirit or removes them from sources of energetic renewal. A diminished sense of satisfaction and vitality are associated with their flare-ups of symptoms. When a Sparkler gets back on track with her joyous life, her health tends to improve rapidly and dramatically.

Suggestions for Sparklers

Pay attention to your dreams, your physical sensations, and your health when you begin a new relationship. You have a straightforward system that will start to feel off quickly if you have taken a wrong turn and will bubble with joy when you're going in the right direction. If you start to feel short of breath, drained, or edgy, pay attention. These are early somatic signals that you're being squeezed of your vitality and separated from your energetic renewal. Make it a habit to be unfailingly honest with yourself and to look unflinchingly at any intuitive signal that may appear.

If you begin to have a recurring dream, write it down and talk to friends about it, and read chapter 9, on relationship dreams and symbols, to get started making sense of your dreams. Your dreaming mind is your best watchdog and will give you important lead time to head off trouble.

Take your time with romance and let things blossom, as difficult as that is for you to do. Allow your partner time to see how busy you like to be and how fulfilling your social calendar is to you.

Be candid about your needs with yourself and others. You don't just like activity and people—you need them to be happy and healthy.

Look for love in friendship. Instead of falling for spontaneous combustion, which is one of your specialties, look for a friend with a warm, unwavering heart. Your best bet is someone who understands your nature, loves who and what you are, and knows that there is plenty of sunshine to go around.

When you fantasize about love, don't focus on the movie star you like, the type of hair that turns you on, or how great it would be to have a vacation home abroad. There is nothing wrong with any of these things, but you don't want to fix them in your unconscious mind. Our fantasies actually become relationship triggers that have a powerful unconscious pull on our feelings. You can find yourself falling for a guy's profile or his wardrobe because your fantasies have created an emotional imprint, and this can give you a strong sense of recognition and desire toward someone who has the elements of your fantasy. Instead, fantasize about your own good feelings, of being appreciated and accepted, of having someone who praises you and cheers for you. (You don't have to worry that a fulfilling partnership might not be hot—all your relationships are hot!) Remember, what you fantasize about you will be attracted to. Don't indulge in fantasy about yucky situations or the feisty psychotic romances depicted in movies. Fantasize about what will make you happy, and you will be feeding those coordinates into your intuitive GPS system.

STYLE #2: THE NATURE SPIRIT

The Nature Spirit feels close to animals and to nature. She also has a gift for glimpsing and accepting the deeper nature of the people around her. For this reason, although she may be relatively quiet or even introverted, she tends to be popular and well loved. This personality type is extremely observant of the minor, telling details of others, and because she tends not to be judgmental of others, she is often the recipient of confidences and confessions. People tend to lean into her and say, "I don't know why I'm telling you this, but…" and then relate exquisitely personal details and worries. Because others feel extraordinarily comfortable with her, she may attract partners who need a therapist or who long for healing in some way.

Although the Nature Spirit easily appreciates the golden qualities in those around her, she tends to be a little vague about what makes her special. She needs time alone and in nature, with pets and wildlife, to feel balanced and restored. The more complex and tense are her responsibilities, the more she needs rest, naps, outdoor settings, and peace. She may attract partners who need healing or who are dominant and worldly, who find her tranquil acceptance irresistibly soothing.

A Nature Spirit's Relationship Loop

Jan, a Nature Spirit woman I know, says that relationships happen to her while she is not paying much attention. She thinks relationships are wonderful but feels equally happy on her own. That's partially because, while she likes the idea of a relationship, she often finds the reality more difficult and even problematic. A typical relationship loop for the Nature Spirit looks like this:

- She befriends someone and they grow close, with promising chemistry. She showers the other person with acceptance and affection, spotting and celebrating his good qualities until that person's heart flies open and love is born.
- With her earthy and innocent sensuality, a warm romance blossoms. She is not thinking of commitment.
- In the face of heartfelt intimacy, sweet sex, and true acceptance, the other person declares a full-blown relationship and one-of-a-kind true love.
- She is surprised that this has happened to her yet again. She is forever being claimed as if by an astronaut putting a flag on the moon. She is not clear whether she wants to make a commitment, but it seems to be happening to her.
- She has a tendency to go with the flow in social situations (which confuse her, so she tries to anticipate what is expected). She glides into being part of a couple without really being clear on how she feels about it or whether it is what she wanted for her future.

- She enjoys the celebration, the congratulations, and the attention that go with a new and promising relationship while she fights down a sense of panic and uncertainty.
- She strains to be a good partner and struggles to steal time alone for rest and contemplation.
- Because she is unconsciously withdrawing for time alone and for restoration, her partner becomes insecure and demands more of her time and attention.
- She begins to dream of escaping from prisons, concentration camps, and castles. She fantasizes about some disaster or some fluke freeing her from the relationship. She repeatedly tells herself that the relationship is perfectly nice and that she is very lucky to have it.
- If there are problems, she will leave the relationship or foster its disintegration. If the partner is admirable and the affection is genuine, she may stay for quite a while but feel that she has lost her quiet, her sanctuary, and her time with nature, which is her spiritual touchstone.

The Nature Spirit is almost infinitely intuitive and grasps the truth about situations and people with astounding accuracy. She does not have a good feel for social conventions, however, and often has the sense of being an orphan or a changeling left on a doorstep. The Nature Spirit is very good at feeling a sense of oneness with the divine, with nature and humanity, but she worries about which fork to use at the banquet. She needs time alone the way the rest of us need oxygen, and she often gives up trying to explain this need to others: they seem incapable of understanding how central this is to her well-being and sanity. In partner relationships, she is very giving and accepting, but after spending time together, she also requires time alone to get back to her center.

Like a creature in the woods, the Nature Spirit can be extremely innocent and flee if she feels cornered. She can also be very trusting, and when she accepts someone with simple affection, they feel honored and uplifted.

The Nature Spirit's Dreams

Although research suggests that women dream of indoor settings more often than men do, the Nature Spirit woman is an exception. She often dreams about driving in her car, exploring the woods or seashore, or of being befriended by a wild animal who walks with her or protects her.

When she begins a romance, the Nature Spirit will have copious dreams about her partner. They will explore each other and the universe in numerous detailed dreams. She may have telepathic experiences involving her partner, in which she sees or senses what that person is going through. In early life, she may interpret these experiences as signs of having found her mate. In later years, she will have learned that a sense of seeing into someone else's experience is not unusual for her and is part of her overall lot in life.

Because of her goodwill toward almost everyone, she may be too accepting of serious drawbacks in a partner, thinking they are merely eccentricities. If this happens, she may begin to dream of being abducted by a dark force or an evil person, or even a monster. In these dreams, she may develop a relationship with her captor so that she feels pity for him even while she fears for her safety and longs for her freedom. When a recurring cycle of these abduction dreams occurs, it is time for her to pay attention to the exaggerated illustration that something is very wrong. Her dreaming mind is saying, "You have been swept away, you have lost track, and this is not wholesome for you." When she breaks off the relationship, she will be astonished to find that her friends had long ago labeled her partner as a loser.

When the Nature Spirit is falling in love, she will also fall in love spiritually. Of all the romantic types, the Nature Spirit is most likely to have an active spiritual or metaphysical interest. She may not be religious, but she feels that everything has a spirit, soul, or essence. When she loves someone, she loves his soul and may see qualities in a partner that have never been acknowledged before. Because she tends to be gentle and may be a good listener, some people assume she is weak or unassertive. Although she is not competitive or aggressive, she can be extremely powerful, like a lioness, when outraged. When angered or frustrated in a relationship, she may have dreams reminding her of her own power. These dreams show her riding an elephant through the jungle, walking beside a lioness down a path, or taking the controls of a runaway vehicle.

If this woman feels trapped in a relationship, she will have recurring dreams of moving out of town, getting her own apartment, or even climbing out a window. These may alternate with fairly enjoyable dreams about her partner if the relationship is a good one, and the mix of the two themes can be confusing. What is happening is that her deeper mind is exploring what works and what does not work in the relationship. She needs to be free, not to explore other partners, but to explore her interests and to return to solitude and nature on a regular basis. If she can negotiate regular time off from the relationship, she can stay in and enjoy the partnership.

The Nature Spirit's Intuition

When she is in balance and happy, the Nature Spirit glides through life in a series of synchronicities and magical moments that she notices and cherishes. She prefers to have pets in her home, if at all possible, and the presence of animals relaxes and comforts her. She may be an avid gardener, enjoy houseplants, or live in a setting that backs up to a natural area. When she is around people, machinery, technology, or concrete for too long, she begins to feel light-headed, muddled, drained, and annoyed. Though nothing is necessarily wrong, she begins to feel that everything is out of whack. This is usually her first intuitive signal that she needs to have time alone to sleep, dream, and read. If she cannot get away, she may feel slightly panicky and depressed, even becoming a little weepy for little or no reason. Some Nature Spirit women (who are benevolent humanitarians) report feeling flashes of hatred toward other drivers on the road or people in crowds when they are far out of balance and away from nature. This is an intuitive signal that they have been too long removed from their core and need to negotiate time and room for themselves.

The Nature Spirit is highly intuitive and may even be what some would call psychic. She may have telepathic dreams of others, seeing what they are going through or what is going to happen. The Nature Spirit is pretty clear on what others need but is less clear and less outspoken on her own behalf. Her intuition fires on all cylinders and will become highly sophisticated if she meditates or keeps a diary of her experiences.

When she is in a relationship, she will get immediate signals about the suitability of her partner. She should pay attention to pains in her body, twitches of tension, a feeling that she cannot or should not express herself or that her core needs are somehow flawed or wrong. Because the Nature Spirit may feel a lifelong sense of being out of place in the world, she may approach relationships believing that she needs to apologize for her quirks. Because she survives in the complex labyrinth of social convention by sensing what is expected of her, she may get pretty far into a relationship by "guessing right" what is desired of her and providing it, without being clear that she is creating an incomplete impression of herself.

Although many Nature Spirits are paragons of healthy living, many also suffer from mild degrees of intermittent anxiety, depression, or obsessive-compulsive traits. When in balance, they are free from these qualities, or at least they remain only a memory; when they are stressed, trapped, or out of balance, their problem will flare up. The presentation of anxiety symptoms, depression, or obsessive-compulsive patterns is a strong intuitive signal that they are too far away from their center, should make time for restoration, and should negotiate hard with loved ones for the factors that will restore their luminous spirit.

Suggestions for Nature Spirits

Accept that your sympathetic, mystical style will attract not only people who want to sleep with you but also people who unexpectedly want to marry you or have a long-term commitment.

Learn to respect your preferences, make them known without rancor, and negotiate for what you need.

Find ways that the feeling of not fitting in the world can dovetail with your occupation or your service to the world. This will change the way you feel about being an outsider and make you less vulnerable to other people's riptides.

Accept that other people will probably not fully comprehend what life is like for you, or why exactly you need so much time alone and in nature. They do not need to understand; they merely need to agree that you can have it without conflict or feeling hurt by it.

Practice saying what is, to you, obvious. It is not obvious to others, and they may be very frightened by your withdrawal or your quietness.

Understand that high-powered types, which you attract, need to be guided often, without anger, in learning how to treat you and how to love you. They need to be told a number of times what to do, and each time they will be surprised by what you have already told them before. Be prepared to keep telling them as often as necessary, without reminding them you told them already!

Practice not feeling like a victim. You must get accustomed to negotiating, to giving and then taking, so that you don't feel someone stole your life and you can never get it back again. Give people some warning ahead of time that you are going away to hole up somewhere or are taking a class that interests you.

Don't assume that because you have to explain yourself, to provide your schedule, and to teach others how to treat you means that they don't love you. Even though you grasp an enormous amount of information about those you love, other personality types do not.

Pay attention to your bodily signals of well-being and your stress signals of anxiety, depression, or compulsivity as early as possible. When they flare up, go out of your way to rest and get time alone. If you are having trouble making a decision or taking action, make it your focus to get rest and get back in balance; then you will see more clearly what you need to do.

STYLE #3: THE WARRIOR PRINCESS

The Warrior Princess personality type is strong, confident, and capable. She is often a professional or a successful businesswoman and is likely at the top of her field or in a position of power. She is often athletic and especially in early life relishes demanding sports or hobbies. She is smart and self-contained, grasping real-world situations quickly and making shrewd investments and sound decisions. She likes relationships and sex in a straightforward way, and conquests come easily to her. She is physically and mentally strong; some envious people may speculate that she is unemotional because she tends to stride through life straight to the power center of her arena. However, even though she is not overtly sentimental and may not seem emotional, she cares deeply about her partner, family, and friends. She is simply tough-minded and brave, emotionally rugged, and does not easily cry or share private things.

This personality type may have been closer to her father than to her mother growing up, enjoying active sports and appreciating conversations about business or work. When she marries, this personality type is extremely devoted to her kids and may enjoy cooking, but she is generally not hugely interested in domestic life in the traditional sense. She tends to find her career exciting and rewarding, and she chooses hobbies that provide a thrill and a challenge.

Warrior Princesses are intellectually sharp, sure of their facts, and may be opinionated or argumentative at times. They are not angry types, but they may occasionally enjoy a good debate and tend to be confident that they are right. One young man who took his Warrior Princess girlfriend home to meet his parents was mortified when his girlfriend engaged in a heated political debate with his father at the dinner table. Later, he took her aside and whispered, "Don't ever argue with my father like that!" Bewildered, she answered, "But I was right." For her, the debate was not personal, and she meant no disrespect. She simply felt that her friend's father needed to adjust his perspective. However, she was shrewd enough to recognize that the family adored the father and that, for them, arguments were signs of disharmony and rudeness. She made a mental note of this important protocol and, in her pragmatic way, was careful to respect it in the future. One of the great strengths of this personality type (and they have many) is their ability to recognize and respect a nonnegotiable priority in their partner's perspective and to honor those high priorities. She and her boyfriend married and have been extremely happy for thirty years.

While she is single, the Warrior Princess easily attracts partners through her athletic good looks and uncomplicated joy in sex. She may be seen as going through a lot of guys, introducing each one to her friends in her buoyant, brisk manner. But when friends see her next time and ask about her boyfriend, she will scowl for a second (because she is trying to remember who they are referring to) and then say, "Oh, him—I'm seeing someone else now." This rapid-fire process may bewilder those who don't know her well, but friends soon grow used to her rhythm. That said, however, she is not promiscuous, and she is not dating and discarding men because she is neurotic or unreasonable. Instead, this powerful personality does not seem to know herself well enough to be able to forecast the fate of the men who pursue her, nor does she typically look beyond the surface of the men who are drawn to her. If a fellow is attractive, seems to like her, and seems nice, then she thinks, "He will probably do fine." She is more surprised than anyone if he turns out to have some quality that she dislikes, though she will swiftly and efficiently jettison him from her life when she detects the problem.

The Warrior Princess's Relationship Loop

One Warrior Princess I know believes she has finally found her perfect match, and it appears she is right. Before, however, she carefully scrutinized her dates and male friends, considering their good qualities, decency, and romantic skills. She would always embark on new relationships with confidence and enthusiasm, but she often found herself disappointed and surprised. Here is a typical Warrior Princess relationship loop:

- She meets a new man who falls hard for her looks, energy, and confident no-nonsense style.
- They quickly become an item, and she is delighted that he seems almost worshipful in his affection for her.
- They do some serious moves, such as having holidays together at each other's families' home or vacationing together with mutual friends.
- Soon, the Warrior Princess, who is a dominant personality, assumes the role of the leader in the relationship. No one says this, and no one acknowledges it; it just happens.
- She gets a little impatient and a little critical of the man, who starts trying to please her, to bribe her, and to guess what he is doing wrong.
- They begin to quarrel because he feels her slipping away, and it makes him angry and frightened. She feels annoyed and thinks that he is getting a little clingy.
- He begins to ask that they talk about their relationship, to spend time being alone together more, and to ask for reassurance and comfort.

- She begins to wonder how and why she keeps attracting weaklings and realizes this is the beginning of the end.
- Without further ado, she breaks it off.

This personality type is brisk and certain in her decisions. Once she determines that someone does not fit her needs, he is out of the picture. She does not waste time second-guessing or looking back with regret. For Warrior Princesses, it is a baffling mystery that they seem to choose partners who need reassurance. As one Warrior Princess said, "I am so sick of all these sensitive men!"

Of all the personality types, however, when this woman falls in love and decides on a partner, she tends to stick with the relationship for the long haul and to have a relationship that thrives and is the envy of others. One of her secrets is her cool clarity and respect for her partner's priorities, as well as her own. As one Warrior Princess told me, "I make sure that my husband gets his way on the big things that he can't live without; and that I get the things that I need to be happy, too. We build those into our life. We never argue about his love of fishing: he needs that and so he goes. I need to travel and so we travel often. We may negotiate on some small things, make trade-offs, but the big things we let each other have. That works for us."

The Warrior Princess's Dreams

This personality type is not typically vulnerable and often has dreams that focus on her desire to build or create something. When she meets someone who is a good fit for her, she may begin to dream of buying a home together, or even of construction projects. She also has a number of erotic dreams about her partner, and when she falls in love, her reservoirs of sexual energy will awaken in full force. With her vast energy, sharp mind, and true heart, she brings a lot of power to the potential of a happy partnership, and she typically does not have a lot of mixed signals in her dreams. In her dreams, she views a good partner with clarity and love, while other prospects appear in a rather cold or unappetizing light.

If she is dating someone who is not a good match for her, the Warrior Princess may dream she is with someone who is somehow defective or weak. Maria dreamed of a diminutive fellow with a shrunken leg who was following her everywhere she went. When she awoke, she recognized that she had recently begun to feel that her boyfriend was, as she phrased it, "kind of lame" in the ways that mattered to her.

Just as her clarity of judgment is strong in her daytime thinking, the Warrior Princess's dreams tend to be unambiguous in their review of partners. Nicole, who was feeling hungry for sex, went on a date with a man who was attractive but troubled. During their date, she felt disappointed and turned off by his depressing auto-biography, which was the main topic of dinner conversation. That night, Nicole dreamed that she went to have a meal in a restaurant and found that her food was covered with insects and weevils. She quickly pushed the plate away from her, disgusted.

When we eat in dreams, it often symbolizes an experience that we are trying to take in, in the hopes of enjoying it and being nourished by it. When we are offered or try to eat something that is intolerable or cannot be digested, it is the deeper mind saying, "This is not for you." Nicole also felt that her date's personality type was of the whining variety, which instantly bugged her. Her rejection of the infested dinner was simple and automatic, as was her determination that this fellow was not for her. She would rather go hungry (go without sex) than have anything to do with a dinner (a partner) riddled with traits that bugged her.

Because a Warrior Princess is not afraid to argue, negotiate hard for what she wants, or even point out mistakes, she can sometimes find herself learning surprising lessons about the sensitivities of others. When this happens, she may dream of having hit someone or of having broken a cherished object. When she dreams of doing something she would never do in waking life, one possibility is that her dream is exaggerating a recent incident in which she marched confidently over someone else's feelings, focusing on being right instead of slowing down to understand. Mary dreamed of repairing a broken-down fence with her neighbor, but when she looked over at her neighbor, it was her husband on the other side of the fence. She took this dream to suggest that she and her husband needed to mend fences. She also felt that the dream implied that being on different sides of an issue was not a problem; they could coexist on different sides of the fence and respect each other rather than trying to win a disagreement.

The Warrior Princess's Intuition

The Warrior Princess's personality always comes from strength, and her intuitive powers are most recognizable in connection with that strength. Ask a Warrior Princess how her family is doing, and you will receive a swift recount of the greatness of her offspring and the achievements of her relatives. She has excellent survival and power instincts and easily senses how to position herself in organizations so that she can succeed. Others recognize her leadership ability and appreciate her as a formidable ally and a tireless workhorse. She is wired to know how to win, and things like success and making money are relatively easy for her. She also senses danger to her immediate family and may have flashes of warning about her mate or her children. When someone she loves is in danger, she may feel a visceral impact as if she has been punched in the gut. She also has a keen, heroic sense of timing and may actually rescue a family member or loved one at some time in her life.

Her intuition about danger and survival is infallible. When she gets a physical signal about taking a precaution or checking on someone, she should always respect and follow the signal. Her body is her strongest node of intuition, and she is attuned to her gut as well as variations in her baseline sense of well-being.

The Warrior Princess has a keen sense of right and wrong, and her intuition about the care of a child or loved one may well be so accurate that others should listen to her. Mona had a son who had injured his arm so severely that the doctors felt it was necessary to amputate. This plan understandably horrified Mona, but she also felt intuitively that it was wrong and unnecessary. She brought in other experts and argued logically but with ferocity. An alternative was attempted, which worked, and the boy's arm was saved. When a Warrior Princess feels intuitively that a course of action will work, it usually will; when she feels that some danger threatens her loved ones, she will stop at nothing to try to intervene and save them.

When it comes to social nuances, however, the Warrior Princess fails to take advantage of her excellent intuition. Her logical mind is like a powerful sword that carries her through battle, and she can miss subtle signals when she has gone too far or when her judgment has been less than compassionate. If she learns to practice meditation (which bores her), or even to tune into herself while performing household chores or exercising, she will be better able to listen to the quieter forms of her intuition. With practice, she can come to recognize softer signals of insight from her body, as well as glimpses of insight in her mind's eye. Despite the fact that this personality type is not a patient listener, when she learns to listen to her inner promptings, she will uncover a different kind of power altogether, one that will enable her to love more effectively and see those she loves in a clearer light.

Suggestions for Warrior Princesses

Because others are drawn to your strength and certainty, you tend to have partners who are less outwardly powerful than yourself. Because you cannot truly respect someone you believe to be weak, you need to learn how to assess whether your date is strong but gentle or not strong at all.

Although your intellect and judgment will take you to great heights in life, your dreams and intuition will help you to discern what is beneath the surface in your dates, lovers, and partners. You always have a plan and a disciplined routine. Make it part of your routine to review your dreams and tune into your deeper instincts.

Trust your sense of what is right. Although you are capable of falling for someone who is not a good match for you, it is not likely to happen. If you are in love and the relationship is floundering or rocky, something is very wrong. You are hardwired for successful partnering, and if there is something significantly off track, it's time to tune into yourself and trust what you know to be true.

When you feel something is wrong, stop telling yourself it is right. You can actually force an unsuitable match to last by sheer force of your willpower, so pay attention to your instincts. If you are irritable, cynical, eating a lot of junk food, or feeling hard inside, then take a step back.

When you find your mate, take note of your partner's priorities as well as your own. Put both sets of priorities at the top of your list, and use your efficiency to plan how you both can have your mandatory requirements met. Negotiate on the smaller things, trade off, and swap favors.

Make sure not to neglect your need for friends and confidants. You may have a tendency to focus on achievement at work and family gatherings only, with the result that you have few women friends over the years. Even if you take part in a monthly dream group or make friends at the archery club, go out of your way to keep and nurture your women friends. They will keep you tuned into your intuition and your feminine instincts.

Although you are rigorously compassionate in a general fashion, you may neglect the subtler manifestations of kindness. One Warrior Princess told me, "I have always focused so much on being right that at times I have forgotten to be kind."

Some people find you intimidating, so if you want them to open up and communicate honestly, you have to let them know it is safe to do so. Learn to switch agendas in some circumstances to discover what is going on without correcting others or directing the situation.

Look at the way your dreams parallel waking life, and take the implications of your dreams seriously; they are almost always as crisp and clear as you are.

STYLE #4: THE DOLPHIN

The Dolphin personality type, like the highly evolved dolphin, is extremely friendly and intelligent. She is an avid communicator with a gift for conversation. She also understands deep and powerful feelings. She can swim in the waters of feelings better than almost anyone else, and no matter where a conversation goes or what feelings emerge, she is always able to stay present. One of her stellar gifts is her ability to articulate the depths of emotion. Like the dolphin who swims in the ocean but breathes air, she is a creature who must have free access to both emotion and conversation to feel like herself.

The Dolphin may achieve enormous success if her work enables her to merge her gifts of conversation and emotional depth. Oprah Winfrey is an example of a Dolphin type who has used her gifts to create an ideal path in life. Her ability to alternate between genius communicator and emotional transformative agent captivates and uplifts her audience. Another characteristic of the Dolphin personality is a tendency to feel a calling to save or rescue others, and she may become involved in animal rescue or a career path that is larger than life, allowing her to affect large numbers of people in a positive way.

Of all the personality types, the Dolphin may be prone to an on-again-off-again battle with weight and food, although she does not necessarily seem to overeat or make poor food choices. One Dolphin type told me that she lost forty pounds without really dieting when she left an emotionally toxic situation. Her body knew when it was safe and shed the insulation that had unconsciously formed around her when she was in an unhappy environment.

The Dolphin's Relationship Loop

Dolphins crave relationship and intimacy. They do not feel that it is fine to go it alone—they want to share their lives and their experiences with someone they love. Once they enter a relationship, they want and expect to make it last. The Dolphin finds it very hard to give up on a partner. Even if Dolphins are not happy, they tend to stick it out and try to do the giving, loving, and understanding for both parties. One Dolphin I know, Helen, married young and after a few years found the relationship unfulfilling, but it did not occur to her to end the relationship. Her relationship loop looked like this:

- She attracts a dry but likeable man who is fascinated by her emotional intensity and her understanding of the feeling realm. She is socially sophisticated and funny, and her charm and loving spirit are like an open hearth that warms him.
- They fall in love and marry.
- During the years when they are both building careers, they get along well because they are both busy and eager to succeed.
- She is thrilled to be with him because she finds it easy to give her whole heart and to appreciate all his good qualities.
- Under the waterfall of her praise and encouragement, he thrives and succeeds in his business beyond their dreams. She is content to be his supporter while she handily masters her own profession and becomes quietly bored with it.
- She returns to school, gaining more degrees and credentials to do something more with her talents and to make a greater contribution to the world.
- She emerges from school and starts a business helping people with their emotions. Her business succeeds almost overnight, because it is in an arena in which her true talents are harnessed for the good of others.
- Immediately, a rift opens in her marriage. She has grown in a way that changes the dynamic between them. She resolves that she will simply make due with less intimacy in the now cooling marriage.
- When they finally discuss their relationship, it becomes clear that her husband has been thinking of divorce for some time. Although this is hurtful to hear, her emotional clarity tells her that it is right for both of them.

- They divorce.
- She quickly meets a new man who shares her interests in helping others. Their partnership flourishes and they marry, sharing a wonderful life together and helping countless people.

Dolphins often find themselves entering an occupation in which they help and guide others, such as therapy or life coaching. They may also be attracted to the restaurant field, as they enjoy people, conversation, socializing, and parties. They do best when they have regular access to an arena in which they can engage in public speaking, teaching, or expressing their emotional wisdom. Often they have powerful opinions about social issues or politics, but not for the sake of power or politics per se; their touchstone is emotional truth, the empowerment of people, and the welfare of animals. Like the dolphins of legend, reputed to lead ships away from treacherous reefs, these women are natural leaders who feel called to be of service to the world.

The Dolphin's Dreams

Dolphins have an affinity for water, and water figures prominently in their dreams. When they are happy and fulfilled, the water in their dreams will be inviting, beautiful, and a realm of joyous celebration. When miserable, the water in their dreams will be dirty or murky, or they will dream of rivers or ponds that have run dry. On entering a new relationship, one Dolphin type, Clarisse, told me she dreamed of taking swimming lessons and diving into the pool over and over again. She felt that, at last, she had met someone whose emotional depth would enable her to express her own emotional power without the need to disguise or downplay it.

Perhaps because these women understand emotion so completely and live in that realm constantly, they attract partners who are more comfortable in the intellectual and logical planes. In the early stages of a relationship, the Dolphin can do the emotional swimming for both parties, but over time, she may begin to feel as if she is slowly dying inside. When this happens, she will dream of fish that are dying, or of an aquarium that is running dry while hapless fish shudder near death. This is her deeper mind drawing a picture of the way her spirit feels: like a fish denied water. If she chooses to stay in the relationship, she must take rapid steps to immerse herself in other emotional environments so she can experience the fluidity she requires to stay healthy and happy.

The Dolphin personality type is happiest when she is with a partner who loves conversation, as she processes many of her thoughts and feelings by verbalizing them. She also needs someone who is not afraid of big feelings, who will admire and support her adventurous spirit when it comes to oceans of emotion. One Dolphin type dreamed that she was sailing on an old-style galleon alone with her new lover. A storm came up, but together they set the sails so that the ship would not capsize or be pulled off course. She awoke from the dream feeling that she had found the one for her. The dream seemed to suggest that they could be an effective and courageous team, pitted against whatever storms life might bring. They have been able to talk through whatever challenges they've faced, and their mutual love of communication has allowed them to understand each other and to grow closer over time.

In dreams, the Dolphin type will often get strong signals about her emotional well-being from the weather (representing her emotional climate) or from the fate of animals and pets. When she is feeling low, she will dream of pets and animals that are suffering, neglected, or wounded. This is a signal that she should immediately turn her formidable powers of nurturing toward herself and take action to nourish her deep-feeling nature.

Another common dream for the Dolphin is that of unkempt bathrooms and overflowing toilets. When she takes on too much for too long and does not make room for her own well-being, she will have dreams of nasty toilets, which signal that she needs to slow down and express herself more creatively. Whether or not she works as a therapist, she tends to be the informal therapist in her circle, and the toilet dreams will appear intermittently when she needs to turn her attention toward her own needs.

When she is with someone who is a good fit, she will dream of luxurious waters or glorious travel with her partner, a sign that she is connecting with someone who has an inner landscape as grand as her own.

The Dolphin's Intuition

The Dolphin personality type is a walking emotional radar system, and her intuition for feelings is incredibly accurate. She can spot a grieving soul at thirty paces, and she is able to speak quietly to someone on the spot and give the advice and understanding that person needs. Because she believes more is better, she may tend to overbook herself or to rescue too many abandoned animals, with the result that she can be surprised at her exhaustion. She tends to think of others far more often than of herself, and sometimes she gives herself permission to turn inward only when her feelings have been hurt.

Her intuition tends to sweep through her on the circuitry of her emotions, the best-paved highway in her system. She will simply feel when something is needed or when someone is hurting. However, she may be too busy or be talking too much to listen to her subtler signals about what she needs for herself. When she gets out of balance, the Dolphin may start gathering things to her by shopping for things she does not need. When she realizes she does not need them, she will give them away to friends. She may eat constantly to keep herself on the move, becoming unconscious of this pattern or unaware of what she is taking in. She may also cook compulsively, taking plates of food or desserts to gatherings or constantly pressing food on others.

When she tunes into her intuition by checking in with herself, she can see visions in her mind's eye, hear the voice of wisdom, and feel subtle nuances of knowing inside. She is incredibly sensitive and intuitive, generous, and loving. Like water, she can flow into any shape or through any channel and she will be there when she is needed. Her weakness, though, is in letting herself get out of balance, running on empty, or neglecting her health or her personal needs for prolonged periods of time.

When the Dolphin makes a habit of meditating, something at which she can excel, or of using her highly evolved consciousness to double-check her emotional findings, she can have an extraordinary life.

Suggestions for Dolphins

When you see yourself doing too much, buying too much, or eating too much, take stock. These are the signs that you are out of balance. Because emotional truth is your sacred text, you must get clear on the truth of a situation in order to know how best to deal with it.

Harness your highly evolved intuition by finding a system of meditation that suits you. If you can't meditate, then do self-hypnosis, guided imagery, or at least practice silence during a daily walk in nature.

Practice mental telepathy with the animals in your life. You have an incredible affinity with animals; they know you have saved them and that you will do everything possible to help them. Try talking to them mind to mind and notice whether you inwardly hear a response.

When you meet a new potential mate, pay attention to your dreams. Your deeper mind is equipped to read the emotional state of others, and you will already have a sense, on some level, of whether this person is a match for you.

Do not marry someone who does not share your love of conversation. Not everyone feels as deeply as you do, but you simply must be able to have the glorious and far-ranging conversations in which you delight. It is fine if your partner enjoys listening more than talking, but it is necessary that he engage in soulful conversations with you.

In a calm period in your life, make a written plan that is your emergency course of action for your emotional well-being. This plan is what you will do to take care of yourself if you are verbally attacked, bullied at work, or if your primary relationship dissolves. You have plenty of power and intelligence to draw on, but if you are ever broadsided, you can tumble into the depths of your feeling nature and feel swamped for some time. The plan is your lifeboat, and you can follow the steps to regain your equilibrium.

If you are unhappy in a relationship and have been so for a long time, give yourself permission to consider alternatives. You hate to give up on anyone, as you are innately nurturing, but sometimes you need to take a look around the corner and see what life might look like in another form. Your biggest block to finding your happy match lies in staying too long with an unhappy one.

You will be happiest with a partner who has a depth of feeling, loves good conversation, and enjoys people. (He should also be someone who will not freak out when you bring home a stray dog or cat without warning.) You need good food and good conversation at the end of a long day, and your partner should be warm enough to provide a safe haven for your boundless, loving nature.

Understanding Your Romantic Nature Is a Good Start

If you did not recognize yourself in the descriptions in this chapter, then it is likely that you possess a combination of these traits. As we grow as individuals, we tend to develop traits that balance our personalities and our ability to relate and connect with others. The bottom line is that the more you understand your own nature, the better able you will be to recognize whether someone is a good match for you or whether, despite initial attraction, a relationship might leave you feeling hungry, shut down, or alone. Of course, love and attraction are vital, but most people have less difficulty finding those catalysts and more difficulty understanding how their essential nature must be allowed to flourish within a relationship for them to be happy and fulfilled.

Chapter 3

Beliefs about Love

A friend of mine, Kim, who recently became a teacher, had always thought of herself as shy and a poor communicator. However, she is proving to be an outstanding teacher who is never at a loss for words. People think she is joking when she says she is shy. Yet during her early life, she steered away from social gatherings because she believed she wouldn't be able to hold her own in conversation. To Kim, her life seemed to endorse this incomplete belief because she noticed things that supported it, and she didn't register the factors that argued against it.

Many times we believe in ideas that are only partially correct, or even not correct at all. We may not be aware of it or consciously put it into so many words. Yet without knowing it, we behave as if those ideas were true and engage in relationships as if the false belief were a formula for love, thus getting pulled off course and playing out a script of disappointment.

When I was a kid, our family had a friend who was a wealthy man and a nice guy. He married a lovely woman and gave her a huge diamond ring. He continued to give her lots of presents at regular intervals. From my perspective as a youngster, I thought this looked like a pretty great situation. Then I saw them together one afternoon, and it struck me that the wife didn't really like her husband much. Later I asked my mom about this impression and about all the gifts our friend showered on his wife. I was thinking, "How could she not like him? He is so good to her." My mom said something I will never forget: "He is buying her. The trouble with trying to buy love is that you don't just do it once; you have to keep buying it over and over again."

I wondered at the time why he had not simply married someone who could love him. He was a nice person, and it seemed like that would not be such a difficult task. Now I realize that he had married someone who almost loved him, but not quite. This man believed that love did not come freely but must be bargained for. Sometimes the faulty beliefs we have about love contribute to our getting into relationships in which we have to perpetually pay too much for a bad bargain. We might pay by making ourselves small, by becoming informal social workers, by learning not to make waves, or by looking dazzling at all times. We don't necessarily think about these beliefs, but they show up in our dreams, and they may register as discomfort, fatigue, anxiousness, anger, or sadness in our everyday life.

Sometimes we develop false beliefs about ourselves because of factors in our family, early experiences, the way teachers and friends responded to us, or even because of a misunderstanding. Sometimes we have learned faulty or incomplete beliefs about love because we had no examples in early life of people who were in happy relationships. In other cases, the happy couples we knew made it look so easy and spontaneous that we never imagined how tirelessly they worked to support, respect, and enjoy each other.

If we absorb incorrect beliefs about ourselves or about the

nature of love, the pursuit of fulfilling relationships can be more challenging than necessary. Faulty beliefs seem to nudge us toward people who are mathematically perfect matches with what we believe. We dance to the music we hear and only with the steps we know. Being in a relationship with someone who knows the other half of the dance makes it seem right. It can also make the potential for genuine love, all around us, temporarily invisible.

When we search for a partner or long to make an existing relationship deepen, we will have a better chance of success if we do not operate with a faulty view of ourselves. There are also a few common faulty beliefs that can make love unnecessarily difficult. Let's look at some of these faulty beliefs, how our dreams might reveal them, and how to combat them.

FAULTY BELIEF #1: NEGATIVE HALLUCINATIONS

A negative hallucination occurs when we simply cannot see something that is, in fact, present. It is said that Milton Erickson, the famous psychiatrist who pioneered hypnotherapy in his clinical practice, would sometimes cause patients to be unable to see an object, temporarily, while all other things in the room would still be visible to them. He did this to demonstrate the mind's ability to functionally block out the impression of an object even though it was still there.

This phenomenon can occasionally be observed when you lose something. Have you ever misplaced your car keys or some other small item and then looked for them in their usual place? You go about your home, announcing repeatedly to yourself and others, "I can't find my keys!" After looking everywhere and getting more agitated, you might take a break and think of something else for a moment, ceasing the recitation of your mantra that you can't find your keys. Then, if you check again in one of the places you already looked, you will find that your keys now are there.

It is incredibly difficult to find something when you provide ongoing suggestions to your mind that the thing is lost and that you can't find it. In the same manner, it is also difficult to be aware of your gifts and talents, your spark and spunk, your passion and aliveness, if you have been told you don't have them, that they are not okay or you had better put a lid on them. Many of the faulty beliefs that affect our love relationships directly or subtly emanate from negative hallucinations about our own best qualities—the gifts we have that we do not recognize.

Invisible Gifts

As a teacher, I sometimes meet women who were told early in life that they were not bright and who have lived much of their lives in that belief (men experience this phenomenon as well, but I see it most often in women). When these women study something about which they are passionate and for which they clearly have considerable gifts, they are astounded to discover that they are smart! One of the first things I noticed as a young teacher was this phenomenon of invisible gifts. It is as if people put a handful of bright stones in a jar one day and years later were dumbfounded when friends asked them about their collection of diamonds. If you do not know or have stored and forgotten some of your gifts, you might have an ongoing negative hallucination that they do not exist.

WHAT YOUR DREAMS MIGHT SAY

If you can't see your gifts, you may have dreams of discovering treasures, opening forgotten rooms in your house, or rescuing prisoners from exile. Dreams of recovery and discovery are the mind's way of hinting at the existence of facets of the personality that you may have neglected or forgotten.

Unacknowledged Beauty

Another common faulty belief can manifest in the way we relate to our appearance. I know two sisters who are both lovely, but Susie is the anointed "pretty one." Renee, who does not believe she is pretty, will shrug and say, "Susie is the pretty one! I'm good at keeping the books." These sisters are both attractive and both bright, yet it is as if they divided up the goods one day and agreed that each of them could own only one of those gifts. Each sister seems to project the other half of herself onto the other.

Darla, a woman I know who lost some weight she had long wanted to lose, explained to me that she had always considered herself "the fat sister" and her sibling the pretty, popular one. Getting past this belief was, for Darla, a key to changing her lifestyle in the way she wanted. With the overwhelming pressure from society regarding our appearance, it is understandable that we become polarized in this area: we either emphasize or disown our attractiveness, sometimes experiencing a love-hate relationship with our looks.

WHAT YOUR DREAMS MIGHT SAY

Many women report dreams about their appearance, starting in the teen years. As the waves of social programming about attractiveness affect us, we may dream of looking in the mirror and finding some horrific flaw or some embarrassing new feature. Over the years, dreams register our struggles to feel authentic at the same time that we long to be desired and to enjoy expressing ourselves. When we find our footing in life and begin to shine, we may dream of discovering a quality in our appearance that delights us, one that we had forgotten or never noticed before.

During periods of self-discovery, we may also dream of remembering how to fly, which can represent the recovery of talents and spiritedness. In some cases, we dream of gorgeous wild animals, like an exquisite jaguar or a stunning wild horse. These dreams of spiritedness and beauty hint at a mysterious association: it is as if the permission to express or explore beauty in our own way were linked with our permission to use our authentic voice. The glorious animals in our dreams are beautiful and strong, fierce and gentle; they roar and they can be silent; they stand out and they can blend in. These animals are not merely symbols of what we can be—they are reminders of who we are.

FAULTY BELIEF #2: BEAUTY LEADS TO LOVE

Teresa, like many people, believes that the way to find love is to be attractive. She spends a lot of time and money making sure that she looks good, and she does! She has little trouble attracting individuals who want to be her partner, and when a relationship doesn't work out well, she quickly selects another applicant for the position of boyfriend. Because her beauty is the road to love, in her belief system, it is the thing she turns to when problems arise. When Teresa is involved with someone and a difficulty arises, her instinct is to groom herself or to buy some new clothes. Teresa is not a raging narcissist; she simply has a narrow belief system about love. She has done what many of us do: she has taken a short-term tactic (looking great) and applied it as a long-term strategy, a key to success, without considering whether it is an ideal plan to reach the goal in question.

THE TROUBLE WITH TEMPORARY TACTICS

When life changes, when we face daunting challenges, or when we want something we don't know how to get, it is a natural and valuable human tendency to come up with a temporary solution to get us started in the direction we want to go, or to at least help us get by for a while. The unfortunate thing about makeshift solutions or start-up moves, though, is that a little positive feedback or a taste of the result we wanted can confuse us. This partial success sinks into the psyche, and we feel like the temporary tactic worked for us. Maybe it did! But this is like standing on one foot while trying to make your way across a big puddle. You wouldn't stand on one foot for the rest of your life; it's just a momentary tactic before you decide what to do next. Yet many of us do the emotional equivalent of standing on one foot for years because we forget that it was just a temporary measure. Without really thinking about it, we solidify a behavior or an approach that is inadequate or imbalanced as a sustained approach to life.

Making a Single Tactic Your Main Coping Skill Can Create Trouble

Teresa, who believes that beauty leads to love, has a single recurring complaint in all her relationships: the man does not understand her and does not see her for who she truly is. She feels isolated in many of her relationships because she is a warm, caring person with diverse interests and a bright, inquisitive mind. Understandably, she tends to attract men who are riveted by her appearance and perhaps are not interested in more. In other instances, she attracts partners whose minimum requirement in a woman is stellar beauty, who approach her because she meets a standard they find important. Teresa continues to win the beauty contest, but what is the prize? It is as if she exists behind a billboard of a model in a bikini while the man she is involved with stands looking at the billboard, admiring the picture, and relating to it. She sometimes feels forgotten, invisible, and alone.

When the action we take to resolve a difficulty makes it impossible for us to arrive at a solution, and in fact continues the difficulty, this is what I call a perfect problem. It is not perfect in the sense of being ideal, but it is mathematically perfect and will tend to sustain itself unless we change strategies or behaviors.

WHAT YOUR DREAMS MIGHT SAY

In her dreams, Teresa struggles with her belief that beauty leads to love. She often dreams of buying new outfits, carefully matching the accessories, and calculating the impact of an ensemble. In these dreams, there is often a frustrating factor, an interruption or a problem that messes up her plan. (This is her deeper mind reflecting her own frustration.) At times, however, there is a younger, less glamorous girl with her, who is thin, unkempt, and frightened but who has very knowing eyes. This urchin girl is, of course, Teresa's younger self, the child of a single parent who grew up without much attention of any kind. This is the girl she transformed into the knockout babe.

Often dreams will reveal the short-term tactics we have forgotten that we used, and continue to use, as long-term strategies. In Teresa's case, she focused on her appearance to attract attention, and because she craved attention, she mistook that cycle of cause and effect for love. Beauty is a miraculous gift to be celebrated and enjoyed. It attracts attention, desire, admiration, and sometimes sex. But to satisfy her hunger to be known and loved for who she is herself, Teresa will need to expand her strategy, to reveal her personality, to share her inner beauty as well as her outer loveliness.

Teresa is beginning to do just that. She is engaging in volunteer work and exploring a number of interests besides her appearance and evoking the admiration of others. As her realm of interests and activities expands, she has begun to date men who actually like her, who are friends as well as lovers. As she allows herself to operate as a larger personality, to let the different sides of herself live and breathe, she is enjoying her life and relationships in a different way from what she would ever have believed possible.

FAULTY BELIEF #3: SELF-ERASURE IS NECESSARY FOR A RELATIONSHIP

A number of women adopt an approach to love that I think of as self-erasure. When a conflict or challenge arises, when there does not seem to be enough of something to go around, or when they need to ask someone for help, they frequently erase themselves from the situation. They are still there, all right, and they still walk, talk, and interact. But on some subtle level, they decide that, given the other people's needs or the multiple factors involved, the most expedient approach to solving the problem is simply to give up what they wanted so as to take at least one set of needs out of the equation.

The situation might be as minor as not having any dessert so that there are enough pieces of pie for everyone else to enjoy. Or it could mean struggling with difficult home repairs when a woman could ask for or pay for the help she needs. She may allow others to talk about their problems but decline to share her own because she does not want to depress anyone else or she feels they have enough to worry about. In large ways and small, this temporary tactic of women giving up what they want or need to keep things running smoothly tends to turn into a long-term strategy, a default setting in a woman's emotional patterns.

The pattern of self-erasure sometimes stems from early training about what it means to be a woman: gracious, compassionate, and placing others first (although some men certainly practice self-erasure, too). In other cases, these women come from a home life in which another sibling or family member required ongoing special attention or care. In some cases, one of the parents was lost, through death or abandonment, and she had to instantly become a miniature adult, needing little and contributing much. In such a household, in an effort to keep things on an even keel, she was taught to minimize her needs, because, after all, everyone had a crisis on their hands.

Usually these early situations are borne of necessity and not intended to harm or undermine the other family members. No one turned to these women and said, "For heaven's sake, shut up and don't have any needs; I've got my hands full here!" But that was the silent message broadcasted and absorbed, nonetheless. On a deep level, these women learned the faulty belief that to be loved and have their needs met, they have to deny having any needs at all! Of course, when you examine it consciously, this belief doesn't make any sense. How can you have your needs met when your approach to love is not to have any needs? This belief about love can make relationships difficult and unfulfilling.

The self-erasure cycle is associated with the sense that you don't actually exist in the way that other people do. You are somehow not as real as others. Many people who live this pattern are actually extremely successful and effective in the world because they do get a sense that they exist when they achieve something or make a contribution. Their work, their hobbies, and their studies or volunteer activities become very important, because it is in these things that they often get their first whiff of oxygen: they make a difference, not by disappearing, but by being themselves!

Endings versus Transformations

When women who have practiced self-erasure see evidence of their own value, they sometimes leave their relationships; create separate lives for themselves within a civilized, distant marriage; or transform an existing relationship by educating their partners and themselves gradually.

Some of these women have discovered that their partners had long admired their gifts of insight and compassion and were in fact their biggest fans! Although there are aspects of the relationships to renegotiate, such partnerships are often transformed into extremely profound and satisfying connections, because the depth of feeling, history, and recognition of each other are already there.

Because people who practice self-erasure have a clear awareness of the character and behavior of others, for the most part, they tend to know when a partner is incapable of relating to them as a greater self with normal needs. These women may leave the relationship after decades, or even half a lifetime, to the astonishment of many who know them. It is easy to wonder why they waited so long. The timing of the end of the relationship seems to depend on a variety of factors, but the weightiest factor is their expanded sense of self, which comes from evidence of their value and affirmation from others that they exist.

Brenda told me that she felt whole when out in the world—but when she returned home to her husband, he continued to interact with her as if she were invisible or insignificant. In the world she felt tangible; in the home she became a shadow. She would feel, as she entered the house, as if she were putting on a vest that restricted her breathing. It was as if the house itself suffocated her. The feeling of suffocation or restricted breathing without physical cause is a somatic intuition: it is the body physically demonstrating what the psyche is going through.

Not surprisingly, Brenda chose to leave that relationship, although it was almost impossible for her to articulate the reasons for her decision to their mutual friends. To her, leaving felt like a matter of life and death, although she could point to no single thing that her husband had done to drive her away. She was choosing to live fully, rather than to exist invisibly, and the choice appears to have been a good one. Brenda has progressed in leaps and bounds in her chosen profession, helping many people along the way. She found a man who admires her very much, and their relationship is quite different from her former marriage. They have been together some time, and their connection seems to be very satisfying and profound.

Although self-erasure is very insidious and pervasive, once women become aware that they have been functioning in this way and have evidence that they exist, there is no turning back. I have a brilliant friend who used to feel invisible; she said this: "I didn't say much of anything until I turned fifty, but now there is nothing anyone can do to shut me up!"

WHAT YOUR DREAMS MIGHT SAY

People with the belief of self-erasure often dream of attending a banquet where others have plenty but they can never be served— they arrive too late, or there is simply nothing available for them to eat. When stressed in a relationship, these people choose to help others and are dismissive of their own needs or plans. For this reason, they may also dream of being unable to find time to take a shower or a bath, or of being unable to find a private and clean toilet facility. These dreams reflect the sense that in their current life, there seems to be little room for them to express their own needs or to care for themselves.

In romance, this person may attract someone very loving but have difficulty expressing her needs if she is still operating from the childhood injunction not to have any needs at all. Even when she is asked what she wants, she will have a tendency to quickly say that she doesn't care or that she is happy to do whatever the others want. She may secretly have a plan for her day off, but when her partner makes a different suggestion, she will sweep her plan aside and announce that it doesn't matter. If she does request help with something, she will add a disclaimer to the request or try to cancel it if there is any sign of inconvenience or effort from the other party involved. "Never mind, if it is too much trouble," she will say. If she is in a loving relationship, she runs the risk of unconsciously teaching her partner to disregard her needs by repeatedly erasing herself as a real person. She wants, more than anything, to be understood and seen—to register as important and worthy of love in her own right. The pattern of self-erasure (applied as the way to find love) makes it extremely difficult for her to experience the recognition and affection she wants and deserves.

The woman with this pattern runs the risk of attracting a partner who appreciates her low-maintenance qualities. She is a woman who seems to not require much attention or emotional strokes, and for this reason, especially in early life, she may attract partners who are takers rather than givers.

People with this pattern, however, are often highly intelligent and keen observers of human nature. Although they may be unaware of their own tendency for self-erasure, they are good judges of character and are not masochistic. Often they create situations or settings, in work or hobbies, where their unique abilities gain them recognition and admiration. They shine so brightly that they begin to feel seen and to recognize that they are real and that others value them. If this recognition of self-worth happens while in a long-term relationship, they will renegotiate the unspoken contract with their partner, which can surprise the other party if their earlier understanding was predicated upon an apparent lack of needs. If women with this pattern can gently and consistently teach their partner the rules of the new arrangement (they exist, have needs of their own, and will no longer simply erase themselves to ease tension), then the relationship may blossom into something deeper and greater. If, however, they turn on their partner with a tsunami of resentment, then the relationship may disintegrate under the onslaught of anger (which likely dates back to childhood).

Awareness Prevents Mistakes

If you are searching for a mate or trying to evaluate a new love interest as a potential life partner, be conscious of potential false beliefs and how they may manifest themselves in your dreams and intuition. Although there are more false beliefs about the self and the nature of love than space permits us to discuss here, these are some of the most common that impair our ability to enjoy and appreciate ourselves, as well as to establish healthy and fulfilling partnerships.

The good news about these false beliefs is that upon recognizing them, a kind of holistic change seems to occur. When you recognize a false belief, you have the power to change it, and changing it alters the way you feel, think, and behave; the standards you hold; and the choices you make. Certainly, there can be a learning curve to adjust habits, but one of the reasons dream analysis and intuitive work are so potent is that they can help us examine and update our beliefs. Also, there are advantages to counseling and therapy, as well as classes on codependence and assertiveness, communication, and relationship dynamics. Everything we learn makes us more aware, capable, and effective. As we strive to educate ourselves, there is a powerful advantage in reflecting on the core beliefs we operate from, as they tend to ripple outward through our experience in so many ways.

Change Is the Rule, Not the Exception

If you feel you have been operating from a false belief, or if challenges complicated your early life, do not think for an instant that you can't change those patterns and have a happy life. You absolutely can! Many of the happily married people I know had huge challenges in their backgrounds—some even came from highly dysfunctional childhoods. They seemed to take those early experiences and use them as tools to sculpt lives and relationships that were wholesome, successful, and very loving. Maisie, whose early life was a nightmare, told me, "You can stop those negative patterns in a single generation and move forward with loving and enlightened ways." She has been blissfully married to the same man for thirty-five years, and she has lovely children and delightful grandchildren. Although her early life did not teach her much about how to create the life she wanted, she was awake, conscious, and determined to learn. From what I see in the dreams and in the life stories of clients, we are meant to change in positive ways. Our awareness is one of the keys to recognizing what will work and what is right for us, where we feel alive, and when love is true.

Chapter 4

RELATIONSHIP PATTERNS

There is a saying among women: "same relationship; different guy." Another variation of this remark is "same guy; different face." If you look at your past relationships, can you see a pattern? Some women fall for the same sort of personality or feel a strong attraction toward a particular appearance. Others deliberately try to get involved with a different type of person and are astonished when, despite their attempts to move away from their pattern, they accidentally repeat it in spite of themselves. This is disconcerting and frustrating. How can we change a pattern if, when we try to change it, we just repeat the same thing anyway?

TURNING LOVE INSIDE OUT

To have choices about relationship patterns, we need to do three things:

1. Be able to recognize them.
2. See the cause and effect involved.
3. Be free to use a different point of reference as we make decisions.

Your dreams and powerful intuition can move between the default settings of emotional patterns and your conscious everyday thoughts. This wise deeper mind is like a messenger traveling back and forth inside you, bringing you pictures of how your emotions are working and of old decisions that you made about relationships and love.

ROBBIE'S STORY

Robbie is a successful executive. He is attractive, friendly, funny, and nice. He has good investments, manages his money wisely, and has a nice lifestyle. In short, Robbie is a peach! He was always looking for the right woman and never seemed to find her. Instead, Robbie has repeated the same pattern over and over again. He finds a woman who is relatively unavailable to him and forms an enduring attachment with her, often lasting for years. Finally, he wisely declares, "This is going nowhere fast!" He summons the courage to break it off even though he is still in love. After a brief respite, dating women who are available but feeling no spark for them, he will again find a gal who is not available and enter into a powerful but remote affair that will hold him in thrall for a few painful years.

Robbie's Dream: The Separation

In Robbie's dream, he was a small boy, very young, and he was watching his mother get on the train and travel away for a long time. In the dream, he did not understand what was happening, but he knew she would be gone a long time and that he couldn't go with her. He felt sad. He also felt somehow that he had the power to get her to come back home again, but he wasn't sure what that meant or what he should do. He would be a very good boy, though, because at least that was probably going to help.

When Robbie was a kid, there was a problem in his family involving the death of one of his siblings. His mother had a breakdown, and she left the home for an extended time. During this separation, she did get the medical and psychological help she needed and eventually became strong enough to return home, where she was able to lead a normal, happy life. Robbie and his family remember that period as a dark and terrible time in their history, but it was a very long time ago, and the ensuing years have been without drama or trouble. Robbie now has a close affectionate relationship with both of his parents.

See the Cause and Effect

The dream of his mother leaving is something Robbie experiences a few times a year, usually when he is in one of his relationships with a woman who is unavailable. His mother left so long ago that he cannot consciously remember whether the separation was traumatic, but the repeating dream reference to the temporary loss of his mother suggests that he has an emotional imprint contributing to his pattern of choosing unavailable women. There is a connection between the pain of separation with a longing for closeness and what he unconsciously identifies as "real" love. It is as if his love radar is set so that the only women who light up the screen are desirable, yet somehow unavailable (for example, they work in a foreign country and travel back and forth, they are shallow and promiscuous and can't commit, they are married to someone else).

Because of the settings attached to his imprint, Robbie feels that an unavailable woman is right for him because the pain he feels when they cannot be together is the same pain he felt during his separation from his mother. He isn't a masochist; he doesn't enjoy these situations and doesn't set out to create this story over and over, but it still happens.

A New Point of Reference

Dreams are powerful revelatory gifts not only because they remind us of important points in our personal history but also because they provide clues that can unravel the mysteries of our own hearts.

In Robbie's case, the dream hints that as a child, his mother's separation caused him to identify longing as a sign of real live. Unless he has an edge of longing and pain, the love doesn't feel real to him. Robbie wanted to have his mom come back, and he hoped he might be able to get her to come home by being a good boy. He probably was a good boy while his mom was gone, and she did come back home eventually to stay, and they all lived happily ever after. So the other half of Robbie's mythology is that being a good boy works! You can love someone who is gone and if you are very, very good, she will come back to you and it will all be okay.

As Robbie began to explore this pattern with conscious awareness of where it likely originated, he began to have other dreams about his family and childhood. In these dreams, he could see how his parents rebuilt their marriage after the tragedy and how patience, consistency, and commitment helped them to slowly begin again. He also had dreams about his early years in college; about how hard he had worked to get through school and how much he had enjoyed excelling and accomplishing goals through his efforts. It was as if his dreams began to remind him of the importance of qualities such as devotion, consistency, patience, and thoughtful effort. He was building a new point of reference from which to evaluate the quality of his choices.

Looked at from a broader view, the chapter of Robbie's history in which his mother disappeared was brief in comparison with the thirty years of rich and rewarding family life since that time. Robbie began to create a new litmus test for love: Love is always fruitful. It grows and expands, deepens and enriches everything. If a love cannot be fruitful, then it is not real. He now says that although he can feel an attraction to someone he knows is not appropriate, he does not think of this as love because it cannot be fruitful. His search for love has led him to a different type of woman, and they are building a strong partnership together.

Almost There

Robbie's former pattern is something I call "almost there." It is characterized by loving someone who is unavailable, either emotionally or because of some obstacle or circumstance. When you're in it, this pattern feels as if you love someone who is just about right, except for this one thing that makes it impossible for you to ever really have a life together. Thus, it always seems that you are almost there, in terms of happiness and fulfillment.

Almost there is a difficult pattern to recognize spontaneously, because it seems as if you have just had a run of bad luck with your choices of partners. Robbie always thought he was looking for a nice woman to marry and have a family with, and that he just happened to have the misfortune to fall in love with women for whom that was impossible. When he changed his reference point, defining love as something that was inherently fruitful (rather than painfully incomplete), he naturally gravitated to a different type of woman. Patterns such as this are difficult to recognize, but they are not that difficult to change once we have a sense of what has been happening.

KATE'S STORY

Kate is a hardworking, powerful young woman. She grew up in a family of seven children and knows a lot about struggling to succeed, and even to be heard. She has a quiet, intense demeanor, which is offset by her tendency to speak up suddenly and dominate the conversation when she has a strong opinion. She is a dancer who worked her way through nursing school by teaching ballet to children. Her figure, as thin and hard as a knife blade, and her striking good looks made her very alluring to all sorts of young men while she was growing up. She wanted to escape from her rough-and-tumble family, and she often became involved with "bad boys" for brief, ill-fated relationships.

Kate's Dream: Bringing Up the Kids

In her dreams, Kate would see herself as a child among her brothers and sisters, getting into arguments with her siblings, fighting over the last piece of the leftovers or which television show they would watch. Kate tended to be the one who settled the arguments, divided up the food, and sat everyone down to do their homework. Even after she grew up and left home, she continued to dream about her siblings and their scrabbling but loving relationship.

Recognize the Pattern

Kate grew tired of her dramatic affairs with young men who seemed sexy and strong but never seemed able to hold down a job or get their act together. Kate suspected that she liked to have rough edges in her personal life because she had grown up with them. She thought she was attracted to the bad boys because they presented a way to escape her crowded family life, at least while she was growing up. As she matured, she saw that they were actually like the younger siblings she had taken care of in her family—in need of direction and mothering.

See the Cause and Effect

Because Kate is strong, she tends to naturally lend her strength to others. Because she is organized and driven, she wants to provide direction to those who are not sure what to do or who seem to be drifting. Although she consciously thought she was attracted to rebellious boys because they seemed sexy, she came to recognize that the most powerful pull of all was their need for her strength, caring, and efficiency.

A New Point of Reference

Kate, highly disciplined in every way, found that she ultimately could not love a man whom she could not also respect. She stopped dating for a while and concentrated on her career in nursing and her continued interest in dance. Eventually, she began to date a physician who was enthralled by her startling beauty and inner strength. They have a strong relationship, and although they sometimes have arguments, they refer to these as "discussions" and are very happy with each other. She now has the relationship she has always wanted: someone who is strong, lively, and passionate, yet solid and reliable as well.

The Rescue

Kate's old pattern was one that is often referred to as the rescue because it involves someone with great inner strength taking on someone who is sexually alluring but in need of rescue. Although she was drawn to the motorcycles and the bad-boy image, once she started dating one of these young men, she wanted to fix him up and get him on a better path. Kate's family was loving and wholesome but crowded, loud, and feisty, too, and she often acted as a surrogate parent to her younger siblings. Once she considered her urge to help others, she realized that these tendencies are powerful assets in her career. She created a new reference point for defining love: she needs to be able to respect as well as enjoy her partner. She was able to find passion and respect in her new relationship, and they are planning to be married.

NINA'S STORY

Nina has a tendency to perpetually be involved with two men at once. She never gets too involved with one or the other and manages her relationships deftly. For Nina, the trouble is that she often finds one man physically attractive but cannot share her hopes and dreams with him. He is the "body" guy for her. She also is involved with another man, with whom she has a more soulful relationship and loves deeply but does not enjoy sexually. He is the "brain" guy for her. Although she changes partners over the years, she tends always to have a similar type of arrangement with new partners. Close friends of Nina's can recognize the new versions of Mr. Body and Mr. Brain when they meet them.

Nina's Dream: Abandoned at the Station

In Nina's dream, she is traveling with her lover in a World War II scenario. They are trying to escape an occupied country and are rushing to catch a train, which is their best chance to reach safety. As they get to the station and are about to board the train, her lover turns to her and seems to embrace her. When she returns the embrace, she feels a terrible pain and realizes that he has stabbed her in the back with a knife. He steps away from her and watches her fall to the ground. As the blood rushes from her wound and she cannot move, she watches him board the train and the doors close behind him. She lies there knowing that she is going to die.

Recognize the Pattern

Nina is an only child who has been excelling like a little trooper her whole life. She grew up in a fairly stable home, where she intensely focused on school achievements and athletic events. Her parents are both attorneys, and they expect her to follow in their professional footsteps. Nina is more interested in creative types of work, but she is planning to be a lawyer because the pressure to do so is enormous and because she also thinks it is a reasonable thing to do and will afford her a comfortable lifestyle. Her father is a very handsome man, if a little cold emotionally. Nina has never felt she could really talk with him because his focus is achievement and excellence, and he seems disinterested in viewing her as a person with an inner life. Her mom is someone she can talk to; she shares Nina's interest in the arts and literature but feels strongly that it would be foolhardy to try to make a living in those fields.

Nina is very fond of her folks, but their lifestyle has never been one that fostered emotional closeness. Her dream shows a theme of abandonment with deadly betrayal from the person she loves most. Although anyone can have periods in life when this is a strong theme, Nina has had this dream as long as she can remember. The dream also shows her trying to escape from an occupied country to try to reach freedom and safety. Nina's pattern with partners tends to be dicey and incomplete, perhaps in part because she deals with a fear of being abandoned through too much control.

See the Cause and Effect

Nina's dual partner relationships keep her from experiencing abandonment and allow her to stay in control. By loving two men at once, she stays emotionally distant and protected from abandonment. She enjoys conversation with Mr. Brain, and she enjoys sensual encounters with Mr. Body. This allows her to focus on her career path and achievements, which are her priority, and to maintain a pseudo-intimacy (but avoid the abandonment that she experienced in early life). Consciously, Nina feels that she could never find all the qualities she wants in one man because they don't seem to be made that way. When she considers how her dreams of abandonment might be linked with her romantic arrangements, she sees that her relationship pattern is a way of keeping herself safe and in control.

A New Point of Reference

Most people find that their romantic partner cannot meet all their needs, however well matched and in love they might be. Different types of friendships, extended family, work colleagues, and friends with shared interests all can help us to have full and balanced lives. Nina found it striking to consider that her convoluted love life was associated with her need to maintain a safe distance from a partner. In addition, she could see how her early life experiences had created a mythology in her mind that love is always incomplete. Her mom and dad were often extremely busy; they wanted her to succeed but were not often interested in the parts of her that did not seem to lead to achievement. She thought her dad was admirable, but she could never share anything with him. She took her conversation to someone else: her mom. She felt a bit fragmented because the performance half of her was loved, but the artistic half of her was abandoned. One parent was admirable, and the other was easy to talk to and felt most like a true confidant.

As Nina considered this, she began to see that she had really abandoned herself. She could not control what her parents chose to do, and she could see how they made the choices they did. But she can make choices in her own life that do not continue to fragment her. As she considers how to spend her time and how to arrange her love life, she no longer thinks about simultaneous partners as the best way to feel fulfilled. Her new reference point is this: She considers whether she wants to chop herself up, splitting her time and her feelings into separate chunks. If she does not choose to get in a serious relationship while she has her hands full with her career, it is a perfectly reasonable choice. She can certainly see a number of people if that is what she chooses to do, but she feels clearer about conserving her emotional energy and does not believe it is necessary to split her spirit to protect herself from abandonment.

Half a Loaf

Nina's pattern is something I call "half a loaf," after the saying, "Half a loaf is better than none." In her case, she collected two loaves to get a whole one (or so she thought). There are times when some companionship is indeed better than none. But this pattern may become problematic when we choose a partner who cannot offer what we need even when more suitable choices are available. In those instances, the half-a-loaf choice prevents a strong relationship from coming into your life. One of the ways this pattern manifests is when women get involved with married men. They may do this to tide themselves over with companionship until something more suitable comes along, but of course, doing so can prevent them from getting into a better relationship while they are emotionally involved with half a loaf.

The solution to this pattern is to be honest with yourself. Identify what is going on and whether it is what you truly want. At this point, Nina does not want a full-blown relationship, but she does not want to continue with multiple partners and scattered attention either. Knowing about her feelings of abandonment in the past will help her in the future, if and when she feels ready for a more permanent relationship.

WHAT ARE YOUR PATTERNS?

If you seem to see the same type of person or have the same type of problems erupt in your relationships, then you may have a pattern weaving through your love life. Take out a sheet of paper and make some notes in response to the questions we've tackled for each pattern in this chapter. If you have a friend you trust to speak with about this, this is a great exercise to do together.

Recognize the pattern: What keeps happening, either in your choice of partners or in relationships?

See the cause and effect: How is the cause and effect set up? What are you trying to accomplish or protect, and what actually happens as a result?

Get a new reference point: How can you redefine love, how you recognize it, or what is necessary for you to feel safe, loved, and satisfied?

To change a pattern, decide to learn to alter your behavior and your definition of love. Often we expect too little when we could easily have so much more. In other cases, we have expectations of perfection that are unrealistic and cause us to doubt or discard a wonderful opportunity. It takes practice to learn to feel differently when we are accustomed to an automatic response in relating, but we absolutely can do so, and it is worth the effort!

Chapter 5

MUST-HAVES AND DEAL BREAKERS

ust-haves are nonnegotiable traits we want in a partner, as well as factors in our lifestyle that we simply will not do without. Although we will compromise on a lot of things, must-haves are the things that simply have to be there, because they are so important to who we are and what kind of life we want. Deal breakers are the things that make it impossible to have a relationship. For many, infidelity is a deal breaker, although for some it depends on the context and the emotional component. It is important to be clear on a deep level about what you must have in a relationship and what you consider a deal breaker. Although you probably already have a good idea about this, your deeper wisdom can show you, through your dreams and intuitive signals, that there is even more to learn about your feelings in this regard.

Sometimes a bad experience in the past can make you wary of love. But if you review what happened in terms of your relationship needs and what they reveal about what you must have and what you wish to avoid, you will be far more likely to find and enjoy the rewarding relationship you deserve. We learn through experience that what we wish for can turn out to be an emotional dead-end and what we thought was moderately important may be something we cannot do without.

YOUR HEART'S INSTANT MESSAGES

I often hear clients complaining about their choice of partner, only then to reverse themselves and say it is not really so bad or that they should consider themselves lucky to be in a relationship. This habitual reversal of direction in conversation can be a sign that you are not listening to what the must-haves and deal breakers are for you. In your dreams, however, there are flashes of brilliant sanity, like instant messages from your heart that depict what is really going on and often illuminate the path to happiness.

Let's look at a few of these situations.

Mia's Warning

Mia is a woman in her forties who had a dream about getting sterilized. In her dream, she was back with her ex-lover, who did not want any children. She was upset by this but did not want to make it *his* problem, so she sought to get a tubal ligation procedure from her doctor. In the dream, her doctor asked her if her lover might consider a vasectomy, but Mia said that he refused to consider it. She preferred to take on the more involved tubal ligation procedure, even though she was not, in her own mind, absolutely sure she never wanted children. She simply wanted to prevent conflict with her lover, and in the dream, this seemed more important to her than her own feelings about the possibility of having a child.

This dream understandably upset Mia. She did not think that she would make the same decisions in waking life that she had made in the dream, and she was no longer in a relationship with the selfish man from her past. However, when we asked the following two questions, we discovered the dream had a great deal of realistic advice for her:

1. What does this dream show about what you want and need in a love relationship?
2. What does this dream reveal about what you want to avoid, including your own patterns, in a romantic relationship?

These questions allowed Mia to step back from defending her dream actions, and from arguing that she would never be involved with that particular man again. She could immediately see that the dream held a relevant warning for her about her own tendency to bargain for love by making sacrifices that violated her own emotional nature. In the dream, she was willing to let go of her hopes for the future (children) and to end her ability to build a new life (by having children). In effect, this dream showed that Mia might be willing to make compromises that were too costly, too important, and too permanent in return for the attention of someone who did not truly love her.

Although Mia had this dream when she was between relationships, it arose with startling pain and haunted her. She said that what she must have in a relationship is someone who truly cares for her, not someone who is doing her a favor by being with her. This simple truth gave her a sense of peace and power about her future. The thing that she must avoid and be watchful of is her tendency to try to please, to make huge sacrifices, and to abandon the things that are most central to her own heart. As she continues to digest these messages from her deeper mind, she feels that she is preparing for the love in her future.

The Gag Order

Dreams tend to make the invisible contracts between people visible through imagery. Tammy dreamed often that she was wearing a gag. She would be going about her household chores in an ordinary fashion, unaware that she was wearing it. She would watch herself doing things, and when she awoke, she would wonder why she had seemed to be unaware that she was gagged. She was a rather quiet woman, and she suspected this imagery was referring to her quiet manner. In one of her dreams, though, she saw that her mouth had actually been stapled shut with heavy staples from a staple gun. She was involved with a home builder, and she knew then that the gag dreams were related to their relationship and to the degree to which her voice and expression were not welcome in it. She and her partner had an unspoken agreement that she was there for him, but he was not interested in her thoughts, and he certainly did not want her to speak them.

Not surprisingly, Tammy's early life had contributed to her quiet manner: she was expected to be seen and not heard as a child, and to assume a supportive role without much personal expression. Quiet people seem to attract friends and lovers who interrupt them when they try to speak, and she was no different—throughout her life people frequently cut her off when she tried to express herself. The issue of expression is one that is central to her life story.

Tammy has moved on from the relationship in which she felt gagged, and as she considers partners now, she keeps her need for expression in the forefront of her awareness. Before this chapter in her life, she would have said that she was someone who did not need to talk very much. Now she describes herself as someone who loves to share and express but who also is capable of enjoying quiet and listening. For her, room for expression is a must-have in a relationship, and a partner who does not welcome her voice is a deal breaker.

The Man in the Mirror

Ellie was struggling with her relationship. She frequently dreamed that she and her partner were searching for somewhere to make love but could not find the right location. They would be interrupted, or there would be no private corner where they could go, or there simply would be some factor in the environment that made it impossible for them to lie down. One night, she dreamed that they were near a beach at the ocean and that she was trying to find some romantic (but not too sandy) spot for them to make love. She glanced at her partner admiringly, as he was very handsome, and reached for his hand. He didn't take her hand though, as he never noticed it. He was busy looking at himself in a hand mirror he was holding in front of him as they walked, turning his head slightly to admire his profile. She turned away, looking first at the seashore and then down the path she had been taking to search for a romantic spot.

Ellie had been devoting herself to her partner, who was very happy with her devotion. He was a somewhat famous celebrity, who was a nice person, but his focus was always on himself and his public image. Their unspoken contract was that he would love himself, she would love him, and he would allow her to love him. She had not consciously thought about this as "the deal," but her dream at the beach showed that this was why she felt so depressed in their relationship, even though her friends envied her and everybody thought he was a great guy. He was a great guy, but he was in love with himself—not her. In the dream, she was reaching out to him, but he was oblivious, admiring himself.

Dreams are often set at the seashore when we have reached the end of one chapter and are opening up to something new. Ellie's dream ended as she looked at the open sea and the horizon, which suggests a new chapter, and she looked at the path of continued struggle to find a way that they could be together. She was at a turning point.

The message from her heart was simple. This is a man who is not ready to look beyond himself at this point in his life. Every time Ellie felt disappointed in him, she told herself not to be selfish. But the dreaming mind lives beyond the censor's reach, and it lobbed a message over the fence to her. She did not instantly break up with her partner, but she settled into her truth, allowing herself the luxury of acknowledging how she really felt. Over time, they mutually agreed that they were not happy together and ended the relationship smoothly.

The man-in-the-mirror dream helped her to realize that she needs to be an equal partner in a relationship, that not being one is a deal breaker for her, and that she is entitled to be the beloved one, as well as the one who loves.

Seven Brothers

Karen began dating a man she liked very much, and shortly after they met, she dreamed that she was going to a family reunion. At the reunion, she met seven brothers from whom she had been estranged since childhood. All the men were tall and strong, friendly, and they teased her in a loving way. She was overjoyed to be reunited with them, and they all vowed to remain in touch. She wondered how different her life would be now that she had so many siblings and how great it would be to share in all their lives— she would have so many nieces and nephews. It was a wonderful surprise and she felt connected with these powerful relatives, who would now always be part of her life. In waking life, this woman had no brothers but had always wished for some when she was growing up.

This was a dream of connection and celebration. The new man in her life had awakened a sense of connection to male energy, in part because their relationship held so much promise but also because she felt supported in a new way. The arrival of fictitious relatives in a dream, particularly brothers, is fairly common for women when they are feeling a sense of integration. Women particularly want to feel a sense of connection, not only with those they love but also within themselves. The dream family members with whom we reunite represent parts of ourselves that we are connecting with and enjoying in a new way.

One of the magical gifts of romantic partnership is the way it can support a better relationship with oneself and provide a safe haven in which to reconnect and blossom. The arrival of the loving brothers in Karen's dream also signaled a sense of friendship as well as romance in her new relationship, which for her have become must-haves for a solid relationship. So far, this dream seems to have been a good predictor of her relationship to come, as they remain together and their relationship is flourishing.

WHAT ARE YOUR MUST-HAVES AND DEAL BREAKERS?

Sometimes the things we believe we want in a relationship are external. Women often tell me that they could never be attracted to a man who had a certain type of appearance, for example. We tend to be less clear on how we want to feel in a relationship, what we need to be able to share, or how much we want to be known and valued for ourselves. It is worthwhile to take the time to make a list of what you believe you must have in a happy relationship, including the internal things. I know a number of powerful women who once believed they had to have a partner who was as successful as they were, but they later found such a partner did not bring them happiness. Instead, they found that what they had to have was a good, solid person who would be a dedicated partner. They did not have to be half of a power couple after all. Each of these women married someone they called "the nicest man I have ever met" and found real happiness.

When you make a list of the things you want on the outside, be sure to make a list of the qualities that make you happy inside as well.

Chapter 6

DREAMING YOUR FUTURE

*I*n this chapter, we look at dreams about the future and how these glimpses of possible future events can serve as navigational guideposts, or at least checkpoints, for consideration.

In speaking with dreamers over the past few decades, I have found many who reported precognitive dreams, that is, dreams that have come true. The most common of these dreams are associated with warnings of danger that later proved true. The second most common of these dreams comes from women who dreamed they were pregnant before they knew for sure and later discovered they were right. The third most common dream is about children: something important happening to a child, or a child being in danger. Finally, some people report that they dreamed of meeting their mate before that person appeared on the scene in waking life. I suspect that many more people have these experiences than report them, as it is difficult to know whom to tell about such an event. It also seems likely that some people who have such experiences may tell themselves that they didn't occur, because the idea of dreaming something before it happens seems too incredible.

Scenes of the future in dreams are controversial, and some people feel strongly that the phenomenon of dreaming the future is not possible, that any serious discussion of these dreams is an insult to their faith or to what they believe about science or the mind. Most people are relatively skeptical about the possibility of seeing the future in a dream, until it happens to them. Anecdotally, however, those of us who work with large numbers of people and their dreams know that such events do occur, even though adequate explanations of the mechanisms at work remain sketchy. For example, we have not yet explored the reaches of our cognitive abilities, and precognitive dreams are a natural part of those abilities. My working theory is that our dreams seem to have flares of recognition when we reach important crossroads in life: a marriage, the birth of a child, discovering our life's work, or the potential for a loss in the family. Perhaps at the level of the soul, we know something of these important junctures in life, not because they are set in the immovable granite of fate, but because they are main intersections on the map of our lives. We do have free will about what we do with this information and what path we choose, of course. But these flashes of a potential future are intriguing clues about the possibilities a relationship presents.

I have spent countless hours discussing precognitive dreams with people who have had them. They are highly credible people who do not dramatize the stories or seek attention in any way.

My Story

In the late 1980s, I was working a late shift and needed to take a daily nap to make sure that I got enough sleep and felt rested for work. To facilitate getting to sleep in the daytime, I began listening to guided-meditation recordings to relax. I would fall asleep quite readily when the recording concluded and shut itself off. During those naps, I began to have memorable dreams that were different from my typical dreams. These dreams were metallic looking, as if they had been filmed with a special cinematic technique; they were black and white, yet shiny and glowing, almost silvery. The content of these dreams was not particularly important, or so I thought, until I noticed a strange thing happening. In waking life, I would run into characters from my nap dreams on a regular basis. If I dreamed of someone I had never met before (presumably a fictional character), that person would later come into my workplace or appear at a friend's party.

After a few weeks, I realized that I was having regular glimpses of the future in these silvery dreams. If a dream was in my standard visual style, it didn't give me such glimpses, but if it had that metallic character, then someone from the dream or some element of it would appear shortly in my waking life. This experience continues to this day, and I am particularly prone to dreaming of new students whom I recognize when the class meets for the first time.

TYPES OF PRECOGNITIVE RELATIONSHIP DREAMS

From precognitive dreams, we can learn about our capacity to recognize love and meet it in a way that is constructive.

THE ANNOUNCEMENT

Several people have reported a type of announcement dream in which someone they didn't know appeared to them, and a narrator told them that this person would be their husband or wife. People who have a tendency toward precognitive dreams often hear a voice or a narrator who explains events as they go along, in a manner similar to the narration that accompanies a documentary on television. For these individuals, the narration is a marker of a special type of dream, so they tend to record them or track them for subsequent confirmation.

Another form of the announcement dream involves a dream character who makes a declarative statement in the midst of the dream. The dreamer typically is in the early stage of dating a new person and has a dream about that person. At some point in the dream, another friend, a relative, or a co-worker turns to the dreamer and says, "He is in love with you. You two are going to be married, you know." Although this sounds exciting, the people who have experienced these dreams described their feelings as calm, certain, and contented rather than excited. The hallmark of these experiences seems to be a kind of peacefulness. These dreamers did not feel that they had to do anything special; they were not concerned about whether the dream came true. They were intrigued and found it memorable, but there was sense of tranquillity involved. When we think about the possibility of glimpsing our future, we may be very excited about it, but when we actually glimpse our future, the associated quality is more often peace, a kind of inner spaciousness, and nonattachment.

FUTURE FLASH

A number of people have described future-flash dreams in which they are married or involved with someone, and then they believe they wake up (though they are still in the dream) and roll over in bed and study their mate. In these false awakenings, they can see the familiar curve of that person's profile in sleep and the familiar furniture of their bedroom. Many noted a particular quality of their mate's appearance, such as vivid red hair or a scar on the person's shoulder. When they roll over, it is an almost mundane middle-of-the-night or early morning awakening. They think briefly about what is going on in current events and their life or the plans they have for the day. When they return to (real) waking life, they remember the dream because, of course, they are not married or involved, and their bedroom, home, and current life are quite different. For all intents and purposes, the experience of the dream was rather like waking up in their future bedroom with their future spouse and future life.

It's not a particularly spectacular experience, just one of those dreams in which the dreamer seems to have a different life—until, of course, the dreamer meets the person from the dream in waking life. Most people say they recognize their dream mate either immediately or fairly quickly after they begin dating. Most of them also say that they did not tell their possible mate about future flash because there was no way to sound intelligent and sane and recount the incident. Some people say that they did not really recall the incident until something in their relationship triggered a déjà vu moment in which they recalled the dream.

Randy dreamed of being married to a dark-haired woman whom he did not know in real life. In the dream, he awoke with his wife and stared at her as she slept. In the dream, they had survived a separation in their marriage, and he was thrilled and relieved that they were back together. He knew that everything was going to be all right now and that they would spend the rest of their lives together.

In waking life, Randy was not dating and was focusing on his career and his interests. After a time, he began to think about marriage and felt he was ready for a serious relationship. Not long after that, a lovely young woman walked into a workshop he was taking and began looking at some paintings he had produced. He stared at her not only because she was looking at his work but also because she was the woman from his dream. Her long black hair and serene features were unmistakable. He felt a frisson of unreality for a few seconds and then approached her. They struck up an easy conversation with quick rapport. He wisely did not tell her about his dream at that point, because he believed it would make him sound like a nut. They dated and married happily.

Later, because of his career, they did undergo a separation of nearly a year. During that time, he had moments of worry that he might lose his marriage, but he remembered the prophetic dream that had, so far, come true. The dream gave him a certain faith that they would survive the separation and be reunited. In their case, the dream did come true. They reunited after the year of separation and have been together ever since.

Another version of the future flash is more action based. In this type of dream, people are married and engaged in family activities together with their spouse. They may be having a barbecue or watching their kids play in the park. The dream is not exciting, it may even be mundane, but it is peaceful and memorable. For these people, it may be years later that they recall the dream, which was like an excerpted day-in-the-life of their marriage.

For a lucky few, these future-flash scenes occur just days or weeks prior to meeting their mate for the first time. In these cases, the dreams seem to permit good recognition of their mate.

A Critical Point: Readiness

In an almost offhand way, a number of people report an additional factor related to these precognitive dream experiences, a factor that seems important because it is unexpected and so many people spontaneously include it in their reports. Many of these people say that just before they met their mate, they felt inwardly ready to have a serious relationship or marriage. In addition, several people said that they had engaged in meditation or prayer before meeting their mate, saying they felt ready for this person to come into their life.

In these descriptions, there was again a kind of peacefulness and nonattachment. These people were setting their intention, asking an intelligent universe, or praying to a higher power, saying in effect, "I am ready to make a commitment. If there is someone right for me, let that person come into my life." Certainly not everyone reports this element, but it is something that comes up regularly, often after the rest of the story has been told.

Common Elements

Here are the elements that most often seem to be associated with precognitive dreams of important relationships:

- A sense of readiness, not only of wanting a relationship but also of feeling that you can handle one and have something to give
- A practice of meditation, prayer, or setting of intention
- A balanced, nonattached interest in meeting your mate: not desperation, not wanting to manipulate or get your own way, but an openness without a sense of force
- A desire to meet the person who is really right for you, not merely to get a lover or partner
- An absence of drama or hysteria

When You've Already Met Someone

Many women have told me that when they met the man they would marry, their dreams took on a forward-viewing quality.

Instead of the steamy sexual dreams that sometimes accompany a new liaison, these women dreamed of their future lives: the homes they would have, the everyday intimacies of morning coffee, and the sound of children's laughter in the background. Some dreamers took these scenes to be previews that gave them a glimpse of the feeling tones and the depth of relationship possible with the person in question. Other dreamers believed these dreams were scenes from their actual future together, like a window in time.

Many people do have dreams of a future life together when they meet their mate. These dreams are not flowery fantasies in which every detail is tastefully arranged or the steamy erotic fantasies that underscore hints of great chemistry. Instead, they look and feel like glimpses of future moments in their life together.

Jess dreamed of a sunny summer day when her husband was fixing a problem with the back door of their house. There was a pleasant breeze through the open windows of the house. She was folding blue jeans, small blue jeans, like those a child would wear. That was all she could remember. It was a brief but pleasant scene of domestic life that hinted at the presence of a family. She did not tell her boyfriend about this dream until long after they were married, because she didn't want him to think she was weird. They have not yet started a family, but she believes they will have at least one child because that future scene was so real to her. It felt like a view into the future.

Frequently, though not always, you may be aware that you are dreaming when you experience a scene from the future. This is called lucid dreaming, which means that something in the dream triggers your sense of being in a dream. In other cases, it may not be clear whether you are dreaming, but you have a definite sense that a scene is in the future. Although this might sound preposterous in the light of day, in the dream process, seeing the future seems natural, comfortable, and clear. Perhaps most important, upon awakening, most dreamers intuitively recognize they have dreamed a scene in their future.

Characteristics of Future Scenes

The human mind does have a tendency to look toward the future in dreams, creating possible scenarios based on your personality, your present course in life, what has happened in your past, and what you want for your future. These dreams are often uncannily accurate, seemingly leaping ahead of the reasoning mind and playing out situations that eventually unfold in waking life. I suspect that these future probabilities are one reason people have always talked about and wondered about precognition. Even when dreams are not precognitive, they may be predictive, because of the astonishing ability of dreams to run through probabilities.

In your dreams, you will likely deal with whatever you are striving towards or worrying about. When you meet someone important, your dreaming mind will attempt to sort through aspects of your connection and weigh the potential for happiness the relationship holds for you. With that said, how do you know whether a dream of your future presents a precognitive glimpse ahead, or simply a scenario of probabilities based on known factors? Based on the dream stories that people have reported to me (which they believe to have been precognitive), there are some qualities in the presentation, content, and feeling of such events that differ from more typical dreams:

- The dreams are not like stories but rather are scenes. They look like cross sections of dialogue and activity, like when you are changing channels on a television.

- There is a quality of reality to the dreams, a sensation that they are somehow real.
- Although most dreams are highly visual, precognitive dreams often involve other senses as well: you might feel the breeze, smell something cooking, or hear birds chirping in the background.
- Many typical dreams are either idealized fantasies or challenging dramas. Precognitive glimpses of the future are often neutral and the dreamer feels content. They seem like views without judgment or drama.
- Future-glimpse dreams are generally not erotic or sexual; they tend to be scenes of life together.
- Often dreamers know they are dreaming at the time they see the scene. They may feel that the scene is taking place in the future.
- Some dreamers report seeing themselves at an advanced age, with their elderly spouse (the person they are currently seeing) after a fulfilling lifetime together. These scenes involve a sense of contentment, satisfaction, and closeness.

If you have such a dream, focus on the quality of your experience. Avoid leaping to the conclusion that because you had a dream of the future involving someone you know, that you two are meant to be together. Premature conclusions close the mind to elements that can clarify understanding and aid in making decisions. Do not try to make the dream mean whatever you might wish it to mean, but instead settle into noticing exactly how you felt during the dream and how you felt when you woke up. If the dream scene suggested solid partnership, contentment, good companionship, and loving kindness, then this is an excellent sign for your relationship (whether your mind constructed the dream or whether it was a precognitive glimpse ahead).

Any time you have a dream that you feel might have been a glimpse into the future, write down your experience and keep a record of it somewhere safe and private so that you can refer to it later on. After you have been in a relationship for a while, there tends to be a story you tell yourself about it, like a narrative. This is the official version of events. However, in your dreams, there is a subjective level, another voice that also tells a story. Sometimes the dreaming level of your relationship story is far more optimistic and promising than what you believe or expect. It can be useful to reflect back over a few months of dreams associated with the relationship to see what your deeper mind has been expressing.

Chapter 7

SIGNS OF LOVE

The same brilliant sanity that reflects love in your dreams can also cause you to recognize, in waking life, an aura of something very special about a mate.

LOVE AT FIRST SIGHT

Let's first talk about love at first sight. Descriptions of love at first sight are by their very nature extremely subjective. At what point do you know you love someone? Is love at first sight actually a form of strong attraction that in retrospect, after you love the person, you project backward? There are different styles to our memory, and some people imbue meaning to events in different ways. With all of this in mind, I have come to believe that some people do recognize an important love relationship very quickly and even, as some say, instantly. We know that our bodies have the capacity to instantly register threat on a nonverbal, unequivocal level. It seems that our bodies can also register the existence of a significant connection, even love at times, in a very instantaneous way. This appears to be a form of intuition that leaps into awareness for some people. There are different ways this phenomenon occurs, but here are four categories that are frequently reported.

Captivation: Future Opening Up

One man said that as he saw a woman across a crowded auditorium, there was something about her that captivated him. Although she was attractive, she was not stunningly beautiful, and he was not a man who had difficulty attracting desirable partners, so it was not that he was desperate. Yet he could not take his eyes off her, and he began making his way toward her, dodging people and obstacles. As he walked, he saw in his mind's eye glimpses of the two of them becoming engaged and then married. He saw them having a home together, entertaining and living happily together. All of this opened up like a movie trailer in his mind's eye as he moved toward her.

By the time he reached her and she looked up, he felt a little self-conscious. He couldn't very well blurt out, "Hello, apparently we're getting married. What is your name?" Somehow he managed to introduce himself and carry on an acceptable conversation. He must have made a respectable impression, because they hit it off, started dating, and quickly became engaged. They have been married quite happily for several years now. This man was not someone prone to new-age thinking, or the paranormal. He says he does not normally have precognitive experiences or visions. So when this future opened up in his mind, he could only accept that it meant something significant.

A few people have told me that when they met the person who was to be their mate, there was something special about that person that had an impact immediately. Although we are encouraged to believe that appearance is what attracts us, it may well be some deeper quality in a person that triggers this riveting attention—something we cannot see with the eyes, but that we sense with our being. Not everyone has a tunnel of vision in the mind's eye, but many people say that when they met their mate, there was a simultaneous sense of some probable future. These people are not describing overwhelming sexual desire, or even attraction based on beauty or handsomeness. Instead, there seems to be some quality that captivates their attention. Interestingly, these people all reported something that permitted them to have a certain faith in their experience. Nothing like that had ever happened to them before or since.

It is important to point out that these descriptions of captivation differ from the horror stories of people who have felt drawn into the web of a neurotic or manipulative person who exercised powerful charm or sexual allure. If you have problems falling quickly for the wrong kind of person, then a sense of captivation might not be something in which you should place a great deal of trust or confidence.

Recognition of Importance

Though we fantasize about the love of our life, the real stories of love at first sight are sometimes oddly unromantic. The recording star and actress Cher is well known for her recollection of a strange experience when she first met Sonny Bono, who was to become her husband and recording partner. She said (more or less) that she was not particularly attracted to him and was not smitten, but she saw a glow around him and felt a wallop of significance associated with him. She also said that this was unusual for her. People interested in metaphysics might say that she saw his aura. Yet Cher presumably did not see other people's auras at the time or since. She was left with a sense that he would be important in her life.

A number of people have reported that when they met their mate, they did not engage in romantic fantasies or have visions of marriage. But they did see their mate with a special focus, a luminous quality or a kind of clarity. Some have said they experienced a déjà-vu feeling, while others simply felt a sense of destiny, that the person would be extremely important to them. It was not until after they were dating that they fell in love. In retrospect, they realize that this sense of extreme significance was because the person would become their spouse—though at the time of their meeting, they did not consider that at all.

Recognition of the Mate

A few people have told me that they simply knew the first time they laid eyes on someone that that person would be their mate. Again, this is not based on attractiveness or even on desire. It is simply a knowing. Some of the people did not even want to get married; they had their life in some kind of good order and were not thinking along those lines. Therese said she knew it when she saw the back of a man's head and her heart thudded in her chest as he turned around.

There is often a sense of shock involved in such recognition. The predominant memory is of surprise, not of romance. Diane said she felt a physical impact, almost as if the wind had been knocked out of her, when the man she would later marry walked into the room for the first time. She said, too, that the impact was not because he was particularly attractive to her or because she was interested in marriage at the time. Instead, it was a jolt of recognition and astonishment.

Rapid Rapport, Immediate Affection

By far the most common type of love-at-first-sight story involves an instant liking for the person who later became the spouse. These stories involve the people who meet and wind up talking for several hours after everyone has left the party. These are the people on blind dates who meet and then stay together for the entire next week, announcing their engagement when they eventually come out of hiding. These people report their delight in the other person's mind and personality, and feel they have met their new best friend. They fall into romantic love some time later, but their instant and powerful response to each other is one of rapid delight in the other person, as well as immediate warm affection. Interestingly, these couples also seem to be the most likely to remain together for an entire lifetime once they find each other.

Thought Flash

A few people have reported that when they were reading an online description, opening an email, meeting someone for the first time, or getting together for a date early on, the thought flashed across their mind that they were going to marry this person. (Men report this experience as frequently as do women.) Though women may be more prone to imagining what kind of husband a man might be, the women who report having this spontaneous experience are not the type of women who tend to think along those lines. Instead, the thought seemed to come from out of nowhere, unprompted. One of the hallmarks of intuitive experiences is the unprompted thought that comes seemingly from left field. In most cases these were not people who actively wanted to marry, but were interested in meeting someone for companionship.

CRITICAL ELEMENTS OF
LOVE-AT-FIRST-SIGHT EXPERIENCES

Although it does not happen as often as we might like, some people do recognize the person they will marry when that individual crosses their path. These experiences have certain qualities that suggest something about the ways we can hope to recognize and be open to love:

- A recognition that goes beyond or is not based solely on appearance
- A felt sense that a person will be significant or life changing
- A knowledge that a person will be your mate, without the need to make that happen or to control events
- A profound sense of affection that precedes sexual desire
- A one-of-a-kind experience that, therefore, can be considered significant
- A spontaneous experience, not conjured up or manipulated

Movies, television, and advertising program us to believe that the secret to love is attractiveness. The implication is that we are attracted to someone and then we grow to love him or her. The spontaneous experiences described in this chapter suggest that in some cases, we actually love someone and then learn to be attracted to them.

Love at first sight happens to people who are healthy, balanced, sane, and not prone to being confused about reality or to mistakenly thinking they are falling in love. Because their day-to-day life is consistent, they can absolutely trust their own impression when something extraordinary happens. Like the people who have precognitive dreams of their mate, people who experience love at first sight seem to be unattached to the possibility of finding a mate.

They probably want it to happen someday, but they are not worried about whether it will ever happen.

I stress these characteristics of extraordinary experiences, because it seems that our mental postures predispose us to heightened abilities, allowing us to be sensitive to our intuition and to know when we can trust our impressions. In some cases, we are able to participate in a healthy and wholesome way with destiny itself and invite love into our lives. Let's talk a little bit more about how dreams and intuition can help to better discern whether the person you have in your sights is the right one for you.

INTUITIVE SIGNALS OF LOVE

How do you know when someone might be "the one"? Romance can be anything from a mystery to a minefield for many of us. We are afraid of being hurt; yet we are also eager to find love. Fear and desire are the emotions that make it easiest to make costly mistakes, and this may be one reason why it's hard to stay clear and calm when exploring romantic possibilities. The mind loves to rationalize our desires, and it may start reeling off a list of reasons someone might be good for you or why a partnership could work. The mind can also race ahead with worry and dread, tracing insecurities and warning of doom.

If you notice your mind going into warp speed around the appearance of a potential lover, calm it down gently and try not to take the content of those thoughts too seriously at first. Pay attention to the sensations in your body when you are with the other person or when you are thinking of that person. Do you feel safe or knocked off balance? Do you feel a sense of coming home or of losing your way? Do you feel anxious or confident? Your body is constantly talking to you, letting you know when you are getting closer to happiness and when you are moving away from it. This is particularly true with respect to the sensations you have around the region of your heart.

In my fifteen years of teaching about intuition, the differences and similarities in the intuitive signals people report have impressed me. We have all read and heard stories of people who knew when a loved one was in danger or who sensed danger and avoided harm. In less dramatic style, though, people seem to have a powerful and reliable instinct for happiness and for knowing what suits them on a deep level.

On a physical level, it seems that the body is always sensing whether you are safe or unsafe, comfortable or uncomfortable, nourished or starved, growing or restricted. This awareness is like a yes-or-no signal. Some people say it is like feeling that something is "okay, or not okay."

When you meet someone new who qualifies as a potential mate, your body awareness will begin processing subtle cues about that person and how you feel in his presence, on a deep level. You will accordingly begin to have bodily sensations, subtle impressions, and possibly thoughts that flash into your mind. In one sense, your intuition is as individual as your fingerprint: it is aligned with your personality, beliefs, purpose, goals, and individual truth. What makes your best friend happy may well be different from what makes you happy—your intuition is sensitive to your truth and to your life in a unique way. With this individuality in mind, we can learn about the ways that intuition sends ripples of truth to the conscious mind.

The Wisdom of Your Heart

All the recent talk about the wisdom of the heart is not just talk. We really do have different sensations around the area of the heart when we are happy or when we are sad or grieving. In Eastern traditions, there is a theory that we have an energy center in the region of the heart that opens and closes depending on whether we feel comfortable and safe or threatened and on guard. Pay attention to how your heart feels when you are with your kids or your pets or your closest friends. Typically, you will feel open, warm, and relaxed—as if you can breathe easily. When you face something unpleasant or threatening, you may have a closed-off feeling around the heart, in the form of tightness in the chest.

When you meet someone whom you could genuinely love, you may notice warmth in the center of your chest. You may also experience this sensation when you meet someone who could be a wonderful friend, or even when you adopt a new pet. I have had friends and clients describe the sensation as being an intense liking to the point of love rather than grand passion or desire. Those factors may or may not be present at first, but this heart recognition seems incredibly accurate in assessing the potential for genuine love.

Mystics would say that this is your heart opening to someone, unfurling with love and recognition. Others would say that the subjective sensation of a relaxed and welcoming heart is an accurate signal of the capacity to love someone or something. These sensations do not guarantee that love will be returned in the way you might want or that the other factors that go into making a strong relationship will be there for you. But as a point of beginning, it is an excellent place, because it means that you are not just fooling yourself or being swept away by attraction. If all goes well, you could love this person deeply, effortlessly, and forever.

Wanting but Not Needing

Another sign of love is a rather strange paradox. It's the feeling of wanting to be with the other person but at the same time feeling that you would wish that person every possible happiness even if the relationship with you didn't happen. A therapist friend of mine calls this nonattachment. Of course, it's the last thing we are thinking about when we are falling for someone, but if you find yourself capable of nonattachment, it can be very revealing. The couples I've talked with about the early stages of their acquaintance say that this nonattachment is part of the huge affection they felt toward one another early on. They report that, while they wanted the relationship to happen, they also had such warmth for each other that they were prepared to wish the other person great happiness if fate prevented them from being together.

Admitting this feeling is an unusual experience for many people. In today's world, we are generally taught to embrace this attitude: "Love me, or I'll kick you to the curb." We are also taught that when love arrives, it fells us like a tree struck by lightning, and so we can expect that we won't be able to eat, sleep, think straight, or even breathe without the other person. Although a certain initial preoccupation with your beloved is indeed normal, the sense that you would die without that person or cannot cope if he or she doesn't return your feelings is very different from what people who have found real, lasting love report.

If, in the midst of your excitement and attraction, you can also find in yourself a loving nonattachment, then the chances are greater that you are dealing with real love. The ability to wish the other person well, even if that person doesn't make the choices you would prefer, is a sign of mature love.

Lori was involved with a man in the early stages of a relationship when she got a wonderful job offer in another state. Her lover became angry and demanding, insisting that she stay with him and put their relationship first. Although they talked about compromises, he maintained that he had to come first and that if she took the position, it would be the end of their relationship. The more they talked, the more she sensed that he lacked the depth of feeling for her to want her to succeed and fulfill her own dreams. It was as if he wanted to possess her and to have her, but did not care about her as a friend might, and could not see her point of view or respect her goals independent of his own preference.

She accepted the position that was part of her career dreams, and the man severed their relationship completely. It was as if he was punishing her for making a mature choice, and he refused to even wish her well. Later, she felt relieved that she had made the choice she did, not only because it advanced her career but also because it saved her from investing more time and energy in that particular relationship. She also said that if her lover had been more mature and had encouraged her to follow her dreams, she might have chosen to stay with him because she would have felt more truly loved by him.

If a man insists that he must be the only star in your sky, then you likely are not dealing with genuine love.

RECOGNITION AND DÉJÀ VU

Recognition and déjà vu are somewhat related to precognitive dreams, but in these cases, people generally can't pinpoint an actual past experience. Many people report that they experienced a sense of déjà vu when they met their mate. *Déjà vu* is a French term for feeling as if you have lived a moment already and recognizing that moment as if it had already happened. It is also a term that describes the feeling that you already know someone you are meeting for the first time.

Beth was looking at a list of names on a matchmaker website and saw her future husband's name. She thought, for no reason, "I'm going to marry him." She was not even looking for a husband, merely for her next partner, as she was at best ambivalent about marriage. There was nothing spectacular about the name to make it stand out from the others or to cause her to fantasize about having that name herself. She simply had a sense of recognition, and the thought popped uninvited into her mind. When she read his profile and the note he had written, she continued to have the feeling "this is the one." This man was not the richest or the handsomest among her many computer matches. Still, there was something special about him, as if someone were shining a spotlight on his profile. Beth said that she felt odd, though not in a worrisome way, as if some situation she already knew about was unfolding.

Beth and this man had one of the shortest courtships on record, and all who knew her were surprised. The man was nothing like her previous lovers (Don Juan types), but he was in fact perfect for her, and today they are married and incredibly happy together.

A strong sense of recognition does not guarantee all the elements that go into a happy and strong partnership. But an early sense of recognition is a frequent element in the descriptions of happy couples. It is not so much that they saw someone, felt attracted, and fantasized about a life with that person. Instead, they met someone and felt a dizzying sense of recognition, as if there were a spotlight on the other person, and often an instant sense that they had met their match.

Like any intuitive experience, this sense of recognition is more trustworthy if you do not feel it often. The people I've spoken with all said that they had never had such a feeling before. Most of them were not looking for a mate or were not wondering whether the person they had just met could be "the one." When we are actively shopping for love, we tend to try on imaginary partnerships like we try on clothes in a fitting room. If you are in active search mode, you could conjure up some feelings like these by willing them into place. If you are not thinking about finding a mate and have a déjà-vu experience or a sense of recognition, that feeling is more likely to be a spontaneous effect of your intuition and recognition of something extraordinary.

A CONSPIRACY OF FATE

Fate or destiny seems to play a role in finding love. This is not to imply that we lack free will in any way, but quirks of fate help us along at times to "accidentally" find the love that will suit us best.

One woman I know, Lisa, had just emerged without hard feelings or drama from a long-term relationship that had devolved into a friendship. She was visiting graduate schools to which she had applied and went to interview at a school across the country. The school was not the one to which she was most drawn, but she felt in the interest of thoroughness she should visit it and go through the interview process. While she was there, however, she met a young man who was already in the program she was considering, and they struck up an easy and immediate friendship. They exchanged contact information and kept in touch. By phone, in the days and weeks that followed, they fell in love. She was not a flighty or overly romantic soul; she was a scientist and so was he. Yet, as she put it, there was no escaping the fact that, "even though

I don't know this person very well yet, I already care so much about him." They continued their communication and courtship by phone and computer, and she was accepted into a different graduate school program.

He came out to visit her as she prepared to attend school several states away from where he studied. Neither of them could see how this was going to work out, but neither of them doubted that it would. They continued their courtship long-distance, and their relationship flourished. She took up her studies, and he continued with his, and they visited back and forth. Eventually, he proposed to her and said that he wanted to quit his graduate program and start working so that they could live together where she was going to school and so that she could complete her doctorate. This is what they did. Later they married, and she completed school while he worked and set the foundation for a new and successful career in another field.

Eventually, they moved back to her hometown and started a family. Lisa and her partner were brought together by her interview with a graduate program in a university where she did not wind up studying during the briefest of visits to a faraway campus. Her husband happened to be studying there on a career path that he would ultimately change. Lisa wouldn't study there at all, as it turned out. To people who know them, it seems that the interview and brief visit were for the purpose of their meeting. In another subtle hint of fate, this man and woman were born on the very same day, in the same year, miles apart. It certainly seems that they were born to be together!

Women often sit together and share stories of how they met their husbands. This is not only romantic storytelling; in a deeper sense, it is the study of how fate may nudge us toward love in the most peculiar or unlikely ways.

Pay attention to the ways fate may place love in your path. Although fate is only one piece of the puzzle, it does seem that we are wise to be open to it as a phenomenon and to acknowledge that when we are not clear about the question we are asking, some power is telling us that love is the answer.

OTHER INTUITIVE SIGNS OF COMPATIBILITY

Bodily Relaxation

Although there is always some excitement in a new romance or a potential love affair, most people report that they felt something relax inside themselves when they met their mate.

A Life-Changing Connection

A number of people report that when they met their mate, they did not notice a feeling of falling in love or of incredible attraction. Instead, they noticed a sense of being on a precipice or of moving through a doorway in life, a knowing that everything was about to change profoundly.

A Jolt

Some people say that when they met their mate, or even saw a picture, there was a physical shock or jolt involved. One woman said it was like having the wind knocked out of her for a second, and another said that everything else in the room faded away for an instant. Neither of these women felt an overwhelming sense of attraction or of being swept away. Instead, the physical jolt alerted them that something important might be happening, and later they put that moment of shock into context.

Sense of a Brightened Future

The person you partner with or marry will, of course, affect all aspects of your future. Some people report that they envisioned a positive future with their mate very early on in the relationship and felt that the partnership would be a happy one on all fronts. One woman described this as a sense that the meshing of their lives, interests, and careers worked and felt solid from the early days of their relationship.

Breathing Easy

When something or someone does not fit well, there is a tendency to breath more shallowly around that person. Although the tendency is subtle, you may notice that people who stress you out make you feel restricted in some indefinable way, even if you like them and are attracted to them. People who have successful partnerships report that the other person makes them feel refreshed, at ease being themselves around that person, and able to breathe easily.

Being More Yourself

In the early phase of a potential relationship, the overwhelming human tendency is to try to emphasize the ways in which we are compatible and to minimize the ways in which we are less compatible. This can lead to a feeling that you can put your feet up and really be yourself only when you are not with your love interest. When you meet a solid partner, however, there is often a sense of becoming more yourself and expanding rather than morphing into a lightweight version of yourself.

A Sense of Solidity

Many couples report a sense of their connection being solid and real quite early on. In addition to the joy and excitement of falling in love, they also had a sense of standing on solid ground with each other and of being able to safely build on that foundation.

Mutuality

When people click in the early stages, uncertainty or great imbalances in affection do not encumber their relationships. Both people seem to know that the relationship is potentially serious and life changing, even if they describe it in different terms. In contrast, sometimes people believe they have found true love because they are experiencing something profound, despite the fact that the other person does not share their view. Early mutuality of affection rather than lopsided love is an early sign of a rewarding partnership.

Reframing of Past Romances

Some people say that as they enter a relationship with their future spouse, they see their own past romances in a different light. One woman said, "When I felt real, unselfish love, it made me see that what I thought was love in the past had been infatuation or attraction." Another woman said that encountering a deep love allowed her to stop seeing past experiences as mistakes and to respect her earlier life with less judgment and regret. It was as if opening her heart in the present helped her to feel compassion for her past.

HAPPY COUPLES: WHAT DID THEIR INTUITION SAY WHEN THEY MET?

We can learn a great deal from the intuitive impressions that happy couples have when they first meet.

What we know intuitively is often different from what we think intellectually or what we might have come to be expect in a given situation. We have all had the experience of talking ourselves into or out of a situation by selling ourselves on what we want or on what we believe we should want. Intuition is different from the persuasion of rationalization because it often does not coincide with our expectations or fantasies. The intuitive signals of happy couples, for the most part, came as surprises to the people who described them. These impressions are in some cases less dramatic, romantic, and sexual than expected, yet at the same time are quite profound.

On a hot date, we may expect to tear off our clothes—not necessarily to pour out our hearts. We expect a sense of heightened romance, not the sense that we have encountered a best friend. We expect to feel lost, but in fact many happy couples say that they felt that they had been found. Hollywood may encourage images of being swept away in some erotic riptide, but many people in successful relationships describe feeling more like themselves with their partner, having a solid sense of the other person and a brighter, expanded future.

Intuition Recommendations

If you have not experienced any of the subtle experiences described here, that does not necessarily imply that your relationship is not the real thing. Conversely, even if you have had any of the foregoing experiences, it is not a guarantee of happiness. The value of learning about some of these intuitive impressions lies in an increased awareness of yourself as a multifaceted being. At any given time, you know more than you are aware of consciously. Your body, mind, and spirit have a remarkable depth of clarity about what is going on and what is good for you.

Pay attention to how your body feels when you are with your partner. Notice the feelings of safety, openness, trust, and security, not just the erotic sensations. Do you feel expanded or contracted in your relationship? If you are sensitive, you are likely to see things from the other's point of view while in that person's presence. Later, when alone, you will have clearer access to your truth about the situation. Heightened empathy is a personality trait of many sensitive and intelligent people: don't respond to it by self-criticism or feeling that you are going crazy. Instead, observe what seems clear when you are with the other person and, just as important, what seems clear when you are alone. These are just different sources of information, and if you review them and reflect on what they imply about your happiness, you can trust your assessment.

If the subtle impressions that arise around your relationship differ from what you expect, it is likely that they are genuinely intuitive. Make room, even in the excitement of an early encounter, to listen to your deeper self and make note of what it registers.

To maximize the benefit of intuitive impressions, add them to the variety of ways you assess a relationship. Perhaps because we know so little of our intuitive intelligence, we tend to believe that we should dismiss it as spooky and weird or that it should trump all our reasoning abilities. A more effective approach is to consider it an added value—a different type of intelligence with access to different types of information that can enhance our confidence and support our decision making.

DREAMS THAT SIGNIFY A POSITIVE RELATIONSHIP

Your dreams tend to focus on recent new developments in your life, particularly in the realm of relationships. For the deeper mind, your love life and your emotional fulfillment are huge priorities.

In this level of the psyche, there is nothing more important than connection, love, and meaning. Your dreams will track your search for a suitable mate or take measure of your existing relationship with the precision of a satellite photo.

Dreams trace the outline of your current romantic situation and then compare it to the landscape of your heart. When your current love interest is a match with your essential nature, as well as with your needs and goals, your dreams will give you an encouraging thumbs-up sign. Although many dreams are complex and even bewildering at first pass, others are simpler and more direct. We'll talk more about specific dreams in chapter 9, but the following are some dream scenarios that signify love.

DREAMS OF RETURNING HOME

One dream theme that marks a new relationship as positive is coming home. This is particularly common for people who live in a setting that is different from that of their early life. One man dreamed of going back to his family's farm when he met the woman who would be his wife. Many people report dreams of going back to a childhood home or to their hometown when they met their mate. These dreams imply that sweethearts may come and go, but that your current love interest is someone who could become family. These dreams also help dreamers return to their deepest self in the comfort and support of a fulfilling love relationship.

The dream theme of coming home is often called *the return* in psychological circles, as it represents the mature personality circling back to the questions, the challenges, and the loves of early life. It is a theme that arises when we are making a leap of growth in our personalities and finding ways to forgive old hurts and embrace early potentials with greater confidence. If you have a returning-home dream when you encounter a romantic interest, it is a positive sign, suggesting that the connection will bring about growth and enrichment.

There are exceptions, however. If your childhood was filled with dangers or terrible times and your dream shows you going back to a frightening and dangerous time in your life, then of course the implication is different. Flashback dreams of times when you were traumatized or hurt can be ignited when the deeper mind registers some similar danger, however subtly presented, in the figure of your new love interest.

A good way to gauge the implication of a dream about your early life is to note whether the dream seemed happy or sad, serene or alarming. Don't get wrapped up in trying to analyze every detail of your dream: check the bottom line! If you were back home again, feeling horrified to find yourself there or asking, "How did I get here again?" then the dream presents a warning of some unwholesome dynamic in your life. This type of dream suggests that you should be on the lookout for toxic patterns, and if you decide to move forward with a relationship, you should proceed with caution.

DREAMS OF POSITIVE CHANGES IN YOUR APPEARANCE

When we feel happy and good about ourselves, particularly in light of a new development in our lives, we often dream of delightful changes in our appearance. In a sense, this is a visual movie of the mind in which we say, "I feel good about myself; I like who I am and how I feel right now."

Many women dream of having long, luxurious hair when they embark on a new love affair, perhaps because they feel more sensual or freer to enjoy a different quality in themselves. Others report dreams of seeing themselves in the mirror and noticing how great they look—a certain outfit is particularly flattering, their body looks better, or they notice a change in their appearance that delights them.

Serena, who has freckles and sandy blond hair, dreamed that she saw herself in the mirror and was surprised that she was a vivid brunette with olive skin and luminous dark eyes. She thought she looked very seductive and sultry. She was thrilled with her exotic look and thought, "How come I never noticed that I look like a sexy movie star?" When she awoke, she associated this dream of recognizing her sultry looks as a way of owning the more sensual feelings she was enjoying in her new relationship. She not only was enjoying a new connection but also enjoying a side of herself that she had not paid much attention to or identified with in the past.

The dreaming mind takes sharp notice of the impact a new relationship has on you. If you feel restricted and cautious or uptight, your dreaming mind will let you know that something is diminishing your life and making it smaller! However, if a relationship is making you feel freer or able to appreciate new things about yourself, your dreams will show you discovering wonderful things about yourself or your life.

DREAMS OF A HIGH VANTAGE POINT

In dreams, a high vantage point suggests a clear psychological view of present and future circumstances. In general, the clarity of your view (or the fogginess of it) represents your ability to understand and recognize the nature of what you are going through. Once they have established a new relationship, some people dream of being somewhere up high, like on a beautiful hill or a mountaintop, where they can see a wide-ranging and beautiful view stretched around them. This high view suggests a clear awareness of your surroundings, the role you are playing in life, and the purpose of the people and events in your life.

High-vantage dreams are usually reflections of a sense of purpose and empowerment, a time in your life when you know what is most deeply true and important to you. Any time you enjoy a dream of seeing for a long, clear distance from on high, you are likely going through an important, fulfilling, and meaningful process. If such a dream occurs as you begin a romantic relationship, it is a positive signal that you are creating a partnership that will be lasting and support the deepest purposes and meaning of your life.

Heather, who had gone through a saddening divorce, met a new man with whom she clicked rather magically. Having emerged from a period of sadness and disillusionment, however, she was proceeding cautiously, uncertain of whether she could trust her feelings. One night she dreamed that she was on a high hilltop, in a grassy meadow filled with wildflowers. The wind was gently lifting her hair off her shoulders, and she walked slowly in the long grass, picking an occasional flower to hold in her hand. Heather gazed out at the view stretched before her and breathed deeply, feeling freer and more like herself than she had in years. "Now I am free," she thought, "free to be a woman again." She awoke from the dream feeling that she had been renewed and cleansed. It was as if her deeper mind were telling her that she was free of the past, with its inhibitions and sadness, and ready to move forward in her life as a person and as a woman. She trusted her feelings in the new relationship, which flowed easily for both her and her partner. They eventually married and today are enjoying a wonderful life together.

Although these dreams of a high view are deceptively simple, they seem to represent the psyche's ability to distill our experiences and arrive at a conclusion. The symbolism of being able to see all around you is like being aware of the big picture, the overall scheme of things and the deeper meaning of your life. Heather was not told directly to marry her new lover; instead, her dream implied that she was free from her past, that she could breathe emotionally again and enjoy her life (pick flowers), and that it was okay to feel like a woman again. This scene of closure, relief, and renewal allowed her to begin the next chapter in her life with greater confidence.

DREAMS OF NEW BEGINNINGS

When you fall in love, there is a great deal of excitement involved. Yet along with the excitement and euphoria, there seems to be a deeper, slower movement in the psyche, which is laying a foundation for the life you will be sharing. When you are truly starting a new life with your partner, you will notice dreams about building, buying a home, planting a garden, or preparing land. In addition to dreams about attraction, sex, and excitement, you will also have dreams that show you traveling and exploring with your partner, possibly packing or preparing to move. These preparation dreams are often a part of the gathering of your energy for a new life chapter.

A relationship is more than a love affair; it is also an undertaking and a journey. You will almost certainly have a few erotic and fun dreams when you connect with a new partner, as your dreaming mind will reflect and process the delight of exploring and the pleasure of a new possibility. Pay attention to your dreams when you are with someone new early on. If they are all sizzle and do not include scenes of planning, preparation, or contentment, you may need more time to learn about this person. When your dreams show you preparing for a journey with your partner, preparing for a huge project together, or planning a home together, it is a good sign that you are dealing with a life partner rather than merely a lover or a fling.

DREAMS OF SPRING AND SUMMER

In your dreams, the weather may be entirely different than it is in your current climate. You may see snow in July and dream of the tropics at Christmastime. Dream weather is different because it is highly symbolic of the emotional tone of your current life and because it tends to represent the season of a particular facet of your life. When embarking on something new that holds promise, your dreams will likely be set in springtime. When a particular part of your life is drawing to a close, you will likely have a series of dreams set in winter, complete with snow, which often symbolizes endings or the death of a certain form in life.

Because your dreams reflect your current life situation and explore your feelings and reactions to new events, it is understandable that you will dream about anyone new you start seeing. If you have dreams set in summertime that involve your new love interest, pay attention. Dreams set in summertime have a tone of contentment, ease, comfort, and plenty. It is as if the dreaming mind recognizes the potential for fulfillment and compatibility and reflects the positive potential in dreams set in the relaxed season of summer.

Chapter 8

WARNING SIGNS AND WARNING DREAMS

One of the best ways to find the love of your life is to avoid wasting time with bad relationships. In fact, most of the happy couples I speak with tell me that one or both of them had just escaped a bad relationship when they met! It seems that a disappointment or a phony lover helps us to better recognize the real thing when it comes along.

Typically, if there is something wrong with a new person or a new connection, you will experience more than one of the warning signals discussed in this chapter. The purpose of these signs is not to be pessimistic about the new person in your life; the purpose is to use a combination of experiences as corroborating evidence to listen to your intuition effectively and stay true to what you really want.

These signals can range from dreams that present obstacles to more explicit warning signs. How you apply such warnings and the weight you give to the implications of your dreams is up to you. The value of understanding our dreams and intuitive signals is not in bypassing the normal thinking process but in having clues to broader and deeper information and insight. We can easily miss this expanse of information and insight, which penetrates beneath the surface of events and relationships, in the everyday course of life.

Warning dreams exaggerate a negative trait in someone or something and make it memorable. These dreams and feelings are signs along the road warning of a hazard worthy of caution. Two common dream warnings are of dating someone from the bad old days or of dating a "defective creature."

THE BAD OLD DAYS

The most common of all relationship warning dreams is that of suddenly being back in a bad relationship from your past. In these dreams, you are astonished to find yourself back in one of the worst relationships of your life, unsure how it happened, and totally depressed to find yourself dealing with all the old junk. It is typical for this dream to occur after your initial meeting with a new potential love interest, particularly if you are feeling a bit swept away or if the other person is coming on strong. The dream may happen on a more recurring basis if you are already in a relationship that is floundering or if you are feeling, deep down, that you may have made a mistake.

This kind of warning dream should be taken seriously. This does not mean you must break off the relationship or avoid the new person if you don't want to make that decision, but you should start a dream journal and keep a record of the warning impressions you experience; then stay tuned to your deeper mind. In the first flush of attraction, when someone is charging into your life and showering you with flowers, it is pretty difficult to step back and drop that person because of a dream. It is particularly difficult to trust the dream when the two people in question, the old flame and the new guy, look nothing alike or seem on the surface to have different styles.

Read the Flashcard

Here is one way to understand what is happening: the dreaming mind is not terribly interested in appearances or style. It is not providing a negative emotional memory based on style or looks. It is holding up a flashcard that tries to announce something about the essence of this person or about the nature of your chemistry together. That flashcard might say one word that sums up the essence of this person in a relationship, and if you have already had that relationship with another person, the deeper mind recognizes it instantly.

Here are a few examples of that flashcard: "Controller," "Wants Rescue," "Cannot Be Faithful," "Dishonest," "Wants Mommy." If you have had a warning dream of the bad old days, consider what label you would give to the old flame, to the essence of the relationship you had in the past. Now, keep your mind open to whether the new person has similar traits, and if you spot those traits, be forewarned.

Carol met a new guy who came on strong, and the night after their first date, she had a vivid, depressing dream that she was back in a relationship with her old fiancé. Years earlier, she had been engaged to a charming bad-boy type who had glommed onto her because she was bright, capable, and loving. She was successful, so he could sponge off her, and she took care of his two kids when he had them on visits. They got engaged, and soon he was treating her rather badly. She was drained financially and emotionally. She was bright and strong, and after a time, she registered that she was the custodian of his dysfunctional life, not the beloved woman of a caring partner. She broke off that relationship and swore off bad-boy types for good.

The new person she had met was of a very different style. He was charming, attentive, appeared to be sensitive, and seemed to have a spiritual side. When she had the dream of the bad old days, we discussed its implications. She felt strongly that it could not possibly be a warning dream, because the two men struck her as so entirely different. She was thinking of style, appearance, and mannerisms. Her dreaming mind was thinking, "User Alert!" Sure enough, in short order, the new guy started trying to borrow money from her, he needed to borrow her car, and generally he wanted to use her to his advantage to bolster up his lifestyle. She felt, as most people do, that if you love someone, there is nothing wrong with helping them out—up to a point. Because she had already had a relationship in which she had given too much, she recognized the pattern before the new guy settled in, and she extricated herself from the connection.

Implications of Bad-Old-Days Dreams

Bad-old-days dreams seem to reflect the qualities of a love interest—and the potential for those qualities to harm or disappoint you. Here are a few of the implications of this type of warning dream:

- The new person may wind up treating you the same way as your old flame.
- You may be drawn into a similar type of relationship as the one you had in the dream.
- You may wind up filling a role that you held in the old relationship, such as surrogate mommy, social worker, sexual slave, or victim.

- You may be trapped emotionally in a similar way to the relationship in your past, even though the circumstances and the partner appear to be quite different.
- You may be dealing with a bait-and-switch type of relationship, where the presentation is entirely different from the subsequent reality.

Whenever you experience a bad-old-days warning dream, it is worth taking some time to jot down your thoughts about it and reflect on the qualities of your former relationship that made it unsuitable or painful for you. Be on the lookout for those qualities, and take care of yourself in this situation as you make your decisions.

DATING A DEFECTIVE CREATURE

Another type of warning dream involves dating a creature or a wild animal that reminds you of a human, such as a gorilla or a bear. In a similar vein, sometimes the date is a pathetic monster, such as a swamp thing or Frankenstein, an android, or a robot. In these dreams, the woman has a date with the creature and is struck by the difficulties a relationship with him would entail. If he is an animal, she notices he has lice, a pungent smell, and is not housebroken. How will this relationship work? If he is a robot, what will sex be like with him—automatic and cold, or perhaps precise and logical? In these dreams, the woman mulls over the challenges presented by the animal-man's unique qualities and may try to rationalize how the relationship could work, particularly if she feels he is lonely and misunderstood.

Implications of Defective-Creature Dreams

Defective-creature dreams exaggerate the qualities of a particular person to illustrate a point. Do you really want to fall in love with a gorilla and then try to housebreak him? Do you want to marry a robot and then wonder why he seems unfeeling? Of course, these dreams are not entirely fair to the person who is depicted in such a cartoonlike fashion. But your dreaming mind is not in the business of being fair; it is utterly on your side and is relentlessly targeting things that could affect your happiness.

These warning dreams do not necessarily mean that you can't have a relationship with the person depicted as the creature. They attempt to give you a heads-up that the behaviors or traits you are barely noticing consciously are noteworthy because they are associated with larger issues that may be more significant than you realize. These dreams also reveal that you are already getting drawn in, feeling sorry for the creature, and hoping you can teach it how to behave and bring it into society. If you have a tendency to initiate relationship rehabilitation with your partners, this dream is pointing out that you may want to review that pattern. Many women who have the gift of loving someone despite their flaws possess a nobility of character and generosity of spirit that are admirable. However, they can also find themselves in bewilderingly difficult circumstances, burdened beyond the norm because they have unselfishly taken on problems that are unfair to them. These warning dreams suggest that you beware of the very real challenges the other person brings along and that you keep your eyes wide open in whatever way you choose to proceed.

INTUITIVE WARNING SIGNALS

When you meet someone new and sparks fly, you probably feel energized, excited, and stimulated. This is when you race to your closet and try on a few different outfits, searching for just the right thing to wear. When the potential for love is in the air, or even the stimulation of attraction, you feel great. This isn't a time when you can sit still, assume a yoga position, and tune into your deeper mind. Your thoughts, imagination, sense of desire, and hopes for the future seem to unfurl like a flag, and it seems impossible to slow down. Yet even in the midst of the intoxication of attraction, there are ways that the deeper mind may send up a warning flare. Here are some of the rather surprising warning signals that women have reported experiencing.

Unusual Accidents

A number of women have noticed that in the early days of a relationship that later turned out to be particularly painful for them, they hurt themselves with peculiar accidents and mishaps. They say that, in retrospect, those early painful accidents were harbingers of the pain they would experience within the relationship itself. The subtle connection between their uncharacteristic accidents and their unfortunate relationships may be worthy of consideration.

One woman broke her toe shortly after she started seeing someone who turned out to be very damaging to her. Another woman slipped and cracked her head twice in two days while getting ready to go off for the weekend with her new boyfriend. As their relationship progressed, she described herself as feeling like she was often "banging her head against the wall." Yet another woman fell while climbing the stairs to her new boyfriend's apartment and banged her knee painfully. Another woman told me of volunteering to help her new boyfriend with a construction project early on in their relationship, and she then hit her thumb with the hammer.

Some of these women believe they live in an intelligent universe and that signs are all around us, all the time, warning and encouraging certain courses of action. Susan Shumsky, a popular spiritual writer and teacher, has suggested that when we follow our intuition, things tend to flow smoothly, and when we dismiss the quiet signals of intuition, we tend to run into hazards and experience quirky hardships. Those who have shared these kinds of incidents with me find the coincidences unforgettable because they are not accident-prone people.

We have all had the experience of being distracted by a new lover and doing something silly like putting the saltshaker in the refrigerator. This kind of preoccupation is normal. What is not normal, however, is hurting yourself in the process. In martial arts, there is a concept that helps explain this phenomenon. When something takes away your sense of your own power, your ability to focus, and your ability to execute your intentions, it is said that something *took your mind*. An intimidating opponent or a bewildering environment can take the mind of a practitioner, making that person clumsy and easily overpowered in a confrontation.

Similarly, when we engage romantically with someone who has a negative influence on our personal power, this attraction takes the mind even quite early in the relationship. When this happens, it is almost as if we lose some invisible but real part of our power and become clumsy, uncertain, weakened, and confused. In Chinese medicine, which describes our life force as chi, there are said to be times when stress, behavior, food, or the environment actually reduce our chi, leaving us exhausted and vulnerable to illness. I suspect that the unconscious patterns of another person have an impact on us, particularly when we unconsciously let those patterns into our lives.

A friend of mine who is extremely intuitive put it this way: if you hurt yourself painfully while you are thinking of a certain person or preparing to see that person, the odds are good that there is a connection between what you are thinking and the fact that you hurt yourself. You don't have to go overboard to read meaning into the incident, but there are certain circumstances that make such incidents worthy of at least some consideration:

· You have just met someone or have just agreed to see that person.
· You have other feelings of unease, even though you may also like the person very much.
· You have just reached an important juncture in the relationship, you're about to become intimate, or you are talking about moving in together.
· You are feeling oddly pressured or uncomfortable in a way you can't define.

It is impossible to explain how this phenomenon works or even to be absolutely sure how much weight to give these "accidents." But over the years, I have heard so many stories of this type that I am willing to believe that there is sometimes a connection. It hardly seems plausible that your deeper mind feels it would be helpful for you to fall down and skin your knee. It may be that our reaction to certain people and situations affects our judgment, timing, and rhythm to such an extent that we operate from a different, less effective state of mind. If you are not inclined to accidents and have one (or a series) that is sharply painful, consider whether the accident may be some type of warning. All you have to do is be mindful and conscious as you proceed.

Flare-Up of Physical Symptoms

Many of us have chronic or intermittent physical problems that are manageable once we learn how to take care of ourselves. If this describes you, you may have noticed the way stress seems to promote flare-ups of physical problems. Although any life change can be stressful, it seems that certain new relationships trigger this kind of thing. When flare-ups happen, they are worthy of attention to see if there is some influence, aside from change, that may be contributing to the resurgence of symptoms.

Claire has a digestive sensitivity that she manages with her diet. When she eats things she shouldn't, she experiences nausea and cramping stomach pains. At one point, she impulsively launched into a new relationship with a man who had some significant issues. She immediately started having gastrointestinal symptoms and bouts of cramping. When she left the relationship, the symptoms subsided. In a sense, it was as if her subconscious mind was registering that the man with the issues was not good for her and, as she put it, was "cramping her style." Later, she met a man who was more suitable for her, and she fell in love and married him: she did not have the digestive problems at all in that relationship.

The renowned therapist Arnold Mindell pioneered a type of therapy known as Process Work and has written extensively about the ways that the body sometimes seems to speak to us through symptoms and discomfort. To paraphrase some of my clients, here is one way to think about this: If you have a physical symptom that you have learned is your system's way of saying, "You're getting out of balance, doing too much, or heading in the wrong direction," then make it a habit to pay attention when that symptom flares up. So, if you meet someone new and feel that all is not quite as it should be and your body starts to show the signal that you're getting out of whack, then make note of the combination of subtle signs you are noticing.

Flare-Up of Emotional Discomfort

If you have an emotional pattern that you recognize occurs when you are getting off track, pay attention if it emerges when you launch into a new relationship. A warm friendship that turns to love should make you feel grounded and centered in your life, generous, and forgiving of others. A new "just right" love affair makes most women feel euphoric and connected with their loved ones, happy in their work, and tolerant of others. When the door of love opens, warmth and peace, joy and ease rush in.

If you start a new relationship and notice an almost immediate resurgence of an old emotional challenge, then pay attention. When the psychological patterns associated with fear, depression, perfectionism, and anger rise up, they are worthy of your interest. A new love interest should not make you feel fragmented or disconnected from your own life. If it does, then be cautious.

A Sense of Being Ill at Ease

Finally, one of the subtle warning signals to notice is the sense of being ill at ease. The happy couples I've spoken with all seem to mention how at home they feel with each other, and that this was something they noticed very early on in their acquaintance. They also seem to be good at communicating with each other, trusting that they can be honest and will not be judged or condemned. The best-selling author Deepak Chopra has written of the body's way of registering comfort when we are taking the right path, taking care of ourselves, and improving our well-being. When we are going the wrong way, making a mistake, failing to care for ourselves, or feeling that something is wrong, we feel discomfort.

RELATIONSHIP WARNING DREAMS

Just as your gut instinct can be an incredible ally as you make important life decisions, so can your dreams provide powerful insights. Dreams that reflect stress, worry, or growing problems may seem disturbing, but their startling symbolism helps to get our attention and convince us to take our innermost feelings seriously. Even the most troubling dream can ultimately prove empowering and beneficial, if we understand it.

If you've had a relationship that turned into a huge disaster, you may have wondered, "How did I get myself into this?" In retrospect, you can see how it all began, how it built up, and perhaps how you missed certain signs that make sense from a broader perspective. Certainly, misfortune and disappointment can come suddenly and without warning. There are times, though, when we overlook signals that could have revealed an imbalance problem early on.

Your dreams and your intuition, however, are constantly in the evaluation and assessment mode. This part of your consciousness notices right away that you are losing energy, giving too much, turning yourself inside out trying to please, or crossing a line that is not healthy for you. Because of our natural tendency to adapt and stay in that mode, our dreams become invaluable safety devices, like the fire alarms in our homes.

Here are seven typical warning dreams common to women who are in relationships that are wearing them down or have become imbalanced. These are general themes and, of course, individual dreams will differ. But you can benefit from seeing their characteristics and how other people have found meaning in them.

THE SMALL ROOM

In this dream, you are living in a room that is too small. The ceiling is extremely low and you must stoop so that you don't bang your head on it. The walls seem to be closing in. This is not too bad at first, but as you spend more and more time in this room, you begin to feel sick and hopeless, as if you yourself were shrinking.

This dream illustrates in a disturbing way that the dreamer is living in an environment that is stunting. A low ceiling often reflects the way intelligent and imaginative people feel in a situation where their input is not respected or welcomed. The confines of the room communicate the sense that the dreamer's life—and very self—are shrinking.

There is a subtle dance in relationships, particularly in the early stages, when both parties strive to make themselves desirable in the eyes of the other. Some women are especially willing to read the wishes of their partner and stay within the confines of what makes the relationship work. In a quirk of fate, vibrant and imaginative women are often drawn to men who are highly logical and prefer a somewhat restricted view of reality and behavior. If the woman adapts too well to the preferred worldview of her partner, and even dumbs-down her imagination for him, she may soon find herself feeling constrained in the relationship.

There are variations on this theme, but the bottom line is that of being enclosed or confined in way that is too small for the dreamer. Sometimes women dream of being forced to wear clothes or shoes that are too small for them. One woman dreamed of sleeping with a python that wrapped around her and held her tightly so that she could scarcely breathe all night. Another woman dreamed that her new lover was grooming her hair and nails while she slept and then stuffing the clippings into her nostrils so that she nearly suffocated. All of these variations reflect a sense of restriction, of being forced to live with something that does not fit because it is too tight or narrow.

These dreams do not mean that you have become involved with a psychopath. They suggest that it is time to wake up and examine your feelings of being restricted. Perhaps you need to step out of the mode of adaptation and see what happens if you begin to be your greater self. Many partners are surprised and entirely willing to compromise when they learn that you need less restriction and more room in your life.

If you have spent a great deal of time assuring your partner that you don't need oxygen (metaphorically) and that you are happy in your partner's world, then it is best if you explain things gradually and gently expand your lifestyle. You may have been stuck in the adaptive mode of behavior, but your partner likely did not know this and will be surprised to hear that you are feeling stifled. You will be in a position of stating the obvious (to you), but remember, it is not obvious to your partner. Furthermore, research suggests that high-powered individuals, sometimes called type-A personalities, need to be told interpersonal information several times before it registers. Thus, it may be necessary for you to teach your partner what you need and to have some patience in repeating your story.

If you are in a relationship where you process the emotions for both people, you may feel odd moments of rising hysteria. For example, if your partner retreats into Logicland, growing colder when stressed, then you may unconsciously become more emotional until you feel far more volatile than you would normally be. Don't go there. Stay calm and reasonable, firm but not hostile. If the relationship is wholesome and has merit, you can both learn to compromise and balance things in a new way. If there are fireworks or reprisals whenever you attempt to expand, then you should consider that sign very seriously.

THE DIALING-911 DREAM

A common crisis dream is that of having an emergency, dialing 911 for help, and then being unable to complete the call so that you actually get help. The factors that go wrong differ: some people find that they can't work their phone for some reason; perhaps the buttons and controls are jumbled up. Others get hold of an operator who will not listen or communicate with them or who makes excuses for why help is not available. Some find that the connection simply drops repeatedly and they have to keep redialing.

A variation of this theme is a dream of going to a hospital emergency room or an urgent-care facility and finding that the doctors and nurses will not pay any attention to you. They may tell you that things are okay or give you a diagnosis and recommendation that are absurd and patently wrong. No matter what you do, you cannot get anyone to listen to you. You certainly are not getting any help.

These dreams occur when there is a feeling of crisis: something has gone over the line and escalated to a level of pain that is no longer endurable. The theme often reflects the fact that the dreamers are not paying attention to their own inner voice, which is trying to scream at them. The dreamer is the person dialing the phone and is also the one who is brushing off the situation. This pattern occurs in both men and women, but in my experience, it is far more prevalent among women. One woman dreamed that her clothes were on fire, and in a dream, she asked someone, "Is it me? Am I crazy? I feel like I'm on fire." Part of her knew she was in desperate trouble, and part of her continued to question the validity of her feelings.

The bottom line of the 911 dream is that there is a situation that requires your attention. Take your feelings seriously and seek some help from others. Sometimes this dream occurs for reasons other than relationship crises, but you should certainly be aware of the emergency in your life, because it keeps bubbling up and flashing into your mind. Relationship emergencies include infidelity, toxic neediness, feeling controlled, financial worries, and conflicts over child rearing. An emotional crisis is like a pressure building beneath the surface: it does not mean that the relationship cannot work, but it can mean that you need to look at it soberly and examine and honor your feelings. This is a time to take your perspective seriously and acknowledge your needs and concerns. Once you have brought the emergency into the light of day and sought counsel from people you can trust, you will be able to assess the situation clearly and make plans that are appropriate. Your situation will only improve when you respond to your feelings with respectful attention.

THE BURGLARY AND SEDUCTION DREAM

In this dream, someone gets into your home. Typically, you either let the burglar in the front door, not knowing that he is a burglar, or you become mesmerized by him and fail to secure the house when he lets himself in. Often there is an immediate sexual chemistry between this intruder and you. While he takes some things, he also talks to you, and you both sense that the burglary could end with a rape. You may be surprised that this is not entirely upsetting because the energy of attraction is quite strong, and there is something seductive about the whole situation.

In these themes, the house may represent your life and the intruder a new love interest who has barged in, much to your surprise. The dark, criminal theme suggests that there is something about the situation that you are not clear on. There is an invasion, a robbery, a violation, a crime, yet it is associated with seduction. In some dreams, the woman fights the burglar, despite her feelings for him, and in others, she is enthralled and seduced.

These dreams typically occur early in a relationship, and they illustrate that there is something off-kilter. They often occur when there is an element of violation or psychological abduction involved in the new relationship. You may feel swept away, or you may be seduced by irresistible chemistry, against your better judgment.

If you experience a burglar dream during the initial phase of a relationship, be cautious. Although there is nothing wrong with letting someone new into your life (your house), if the dreaming mind creates a story line of invasion and violation, there may be good reason. Burglary is about a lack of respect, an invasion of privacy, and ultimately theft. Think about it: there is a difference between wanting to give someone something and having that person simply think it's okay to take it from you.

Joanie met a free-spirited man and launched into a casual relationship with him. She found his free and easy style liberating and exciting. Yet after a few weeks, she realized that he assumed that she was always there for him when he wanted and that he took his welcome, to her home, to her body, and to her time, for granted. Perhaps she had misled him by being overly welcoming, or perhaps he was simply a bit opportunistic or unaware. Whatever the cause, when she dreamed of having a handsome but annoying man break into her home and start taking her things, she knew that the dream was highlighting her feeling that her life had been invaded in a way that was draining.

The burglar dreams are not the kiss of death for a relationship, but they are worth remembering and considering if you are embarking on a new connection. You may choose to explore this chemistry and see where it leads, but also take your needs for privacy, safety, and security seriously and keep them in the forefront of your mind.

THE BODY-DAMAGE DREAM

In this disturbing dream, you have lost a limb or suffered damage to your hands. Maybe your hands have been amputated or your feet or legs are gone. You feel strange that this is more annoying or embarrassing than it is painful. You may be annoyed at this circumstance but go about the business of trying to drive your car and get around. You may also feel the need to conceal the situation as best you can from others so that they don't feel sorry for you or make embarrassing inquiries into what has happened.

In most cases, we dream of simply hopping along on our one remaining leg or of struggling to manage tasks by grasping things with our wrists. The dream makes no reference to how the amputation occurred. This suggests that the dream is saying, "Look out, you're letting go of something and the loss makes you feel incomplete or fragmented." If you do dream that someone or something is actually whittling you down, you will want to get your support system involved and ask others if they see something wrong in your relationship. This does not mean that your partner is an axe murderer, but it is a severe warning that something unhealthy is happening and that the cost to you is great.

Body-damage dreams sicken us when we awaken, but it is important to note that during the dream, we may be accepting of what has happened or preoccupied with concealing what has happened. Something grave, horrific, and irreparable has occurred, and at the time, you don't seem to register the horror. Instead, you are busy trying to compensate for the loss and prevent others from seeing your dilemma or pain. Upon awakening, dreamers often feel so repulsed and worried about the dream imagery that they don't want to explore what it might mean.

It is important to remember that dreams depict emotional and psychological events as physical losses and changes. Women often dream of dismemberment when they are feeling separated from parts of themselves that they treasure. It is a kind of soul loss, and it is one of the casualties in relationships that fragment the self instead of making one feel whole.

If you dream of dismemberment, please pay close attention. Avoid getting grossed out by the imagery and don't panic. Your dreams may simply be suggesting a fragmentation of the self that is arising from an imbalanced relationship. As with all warning dreams, the purpose is to get your attention and to encourage you to take this loss seriously. Unlike the permanence of dismemberment, the psychological loss is repairable, and what you have lost can be redeemed.

THE ABANDONED OR ABUSED ANIMALS DREAM

In this dream, you find that your pet has been wounded in a way that was obviously deliberate. You find the pet on your doorstep or retrieve it from a trusted friend's house and find that it has been tortured or maimed. You are sick about this, and unsure if the animal can be saved, although it seems to be hanging on and bravely looks you in the eye as if to say it knows you will do your best for it. The dream is likely to recur in assorted variations, but wounded animals are the constant element.

People find this dream incredibly upsetting. There is something horrible about a treasured pet suffering, and knowing that it was hurt in a careless or deliberate manner is agonizing.

In these dreams, the pet typically represents an aspect of the dreamer. The vivid horror of the dream (like dreams of dismemberment) is a cry for help and a wake-up call. Our pets represent the most loving, loyal side of our own natures, the part that loves unconditionally and gives without limits. This part of us also requires care and nurturance to survive. When we dream that this tender part of us has been viciously wounded, it is time to take stock.

If you dream of a wounded pet or animal, consider what part of your life is causing you pain. Have you neglected one of your passions for too long? Are you involved in a relationship that is making it impossible for you to move, get a promotion, or have children? Sometimes it is not a particular person but your way of relating to that person that generates a pattern of self-neglect. Unlike the dream, the wounding in your life can be healed and the energy you have lost can be restored to you. These shocking dreams stir our feelings deliberately, evoking compassion for the pet we love. As we understand the dreams, we can then turn that compassion toward the gentle, loving side of ourselves. If you resolve to treat yourself with kindness and to treasure your gentle, loving qualities, you will naturally make the right choices for yourself.

THE BLOOD-LOSS DREAM

In the blood-loss dream, you have been injured and are losing a lot of blood. You feel your life slipping away; it's so insidious and rapid that there doesn't seem to be enough time to get help. There is a hazy quality to these dreams, as if you were faint from loss of blood. In addition to the sense of debilitation and fatigue, you're having trouble thinking and tracking things; you may faint or move in and out of consciousness as you try to figure out what you can do about the situation.

Blood loss in dreams often represents a loss of energy and vitality. Women often report this dream when they are in tough circumstances. Think of feeling so drained that it seems you could just lie down and die. This is the background of the blood-loss dream. Often the dream begins with waking up in a pool of blood or getting out of bed only to slip and lose your footing because there is so much of your blood on the floor. In a different presentation, there is a man who has slit your throat—not enough to kill you right away but enough so that you cannot stop the bleeding, and it just goes on and on. In dreams, the throat can represent your authentic voice, your ability to express your truth, and your sense of personal power.

Some research indicates women tend to dream of blood during their menstrual periods. But the dreams of life-threatening blood loss are of a different variety. These are associated with draining people and situations. When these dreams are recurring, they tend to reflect a draining relationship. Although stress, drama, and relationship troubles can, of course, be temporarily draining, when there is a habitual loss of vitality whenever you have been with someone, this suggests that the chemistry between you may not be suitable for a long-term partnership.

If you have recurring dreams of dramatic blood loss, you probably already know what the draining situation is in your life. Kara, a lively teacher, told me that she had become involved with a man who had an addiction. She also had frequent dreams about blood loss. Although he sought help and things improved with his substance use, the relationship was so arduous that it drained every aspect of her life. She eventually ended the relationship, and around that time, her dreams of blood loss ended. Some energy loss is a normal part of life's challenges, but if that type of imagery is ongoing or repeating, it can be a significant warning to take notice. Women particularly seem to get used to living in crisis or putting someone else's emergency ahead of their own well-being. Perhaps it is this pattern that dreams are trying to offset, by showing us graphic and disturbing pictures of a kind of draining that we would never choose to ignore.

If you have dreams of blood loss, even though it may seem impossible for you to do, it is imperative that you start to take better care of yourself and guard your energy as best you can. Limit your exposure to the draining situation, and go out of your way to seek out restorative situations and people. Read positive self-help books, see a therapist, confide in friends, and reach out to your support system. Keep track of where you extend your energy and pull back where necessary. If you have a spiritual life, immerse yourself in your faith and call on it for strength, help, and enlightenment. Though you probably are not in the mood, eat healthfully and try to support and strengthen your body and your health. When we are in such draining situations for a time, we can become emotionally anemic from the loss of energy and feel unsure of ourselves. Fight this, and muster your courage on your own behalf.

As you go to sleep at night, ask for dreams to help you see what you can do to improve your circumstances and to give you restorative experiences as you sleep. This process is called dream incubation or dream programming (see chapter 10), and it is being explored in therapy, education, sports, and business. Sometimes when we request understanding of a challenging problem or an issue that mystifies us, we can get a glimpse of an answer in a dream simply by asking for it. In other cases, even if you do not know what is bothering you, you can ask for dreams to shore up your strength, help you get back to your center, or see the same old issue in a brand new way. If you are feeling burned out, ask for dreams to restore your vitality and enthusiasm or to remind you of what matters to you. The dreaming mind is highly responsive to these nighttime requests, particularly if you are in the process of remembering and reflecting on your dreams.

THE ESCAPE-FANTASY DREAM

In the escape-fantasy dream, someone is trying to get away from a bad situation. It may be you or someone you do not know in waking life. In the story, the person is trying to climb out of the window after dark to get away from her partner, who is holding her hostage in some way. This is a dream that often recurs in a variety of ways.

This dream is a fantasy and a rehearsal for making an escape from a situation that is unwholesome or confining. Women who report this dream are often in a relationship that is desirable on the surface but disastrous underneath the surface. We are often so happy just to have a love relationship at all that it goes against the grain to pay much attention when it seems to grate on us in some way. When we dream scenarios that happen to other people, it is tempting to dismiss the dream as having no bearing at all. After all, it seems like you dreamed about a bunch of strangers—what could it have to do with you? When the situation in real life is a mixed one or when we are invested in the official position we have taken, we tend to dream about a problem as if it were happening to someone else.

For example, one woman who found it difficult to meet men

got together with a fellow and quickly became engaged to him. He was something of a mixed blessing, but her official position was, "Thank God I found a man!" Another part of her mind, her brilliant sanity, was saying, "Hey, this guy is kind of weird, and he's actually starting to scare me!" She began having recurring dreams of women escaping from creepy men. When we explored those dreams, she did not believe they could have anything to do with her fiancé. Sometimes the official position we have about something is too entrenched to make room for the underdog in the psyche that is trying to state its case. Later, however, she noticed things that caused her to leave the relationship. Her fiancé often suggested that they do things and then asked her to pay for them, assuring her that he would pay her back, but then he never did. He would take her out to dinner and then announce with embarrassment that he had forgotten his wallet. Although he seemed to have a good job, he continued to do strange little things around money, none of which was huge individually, but in combination, over time, they caused her to feel exploited. He also would promise to do things to help her and then forget to show up when she needed him, apologizing glibly when she next talked to him about the events that had prevented him from keeping his promise. In retrospect, all of those escape fantasies made sense to her as part of her early process. Her deeper mind may have known, quite early on, that this man was not worthy of her affections.

If you have dreams of escaping from a bad situation, take the time to consider the implications. Sometimes we can feel trapped in a work setting or even a social network. But if your dreams are about escaping from lovers, then the chances are good that the dreams are related to your personal life. If you are inclined to journal, it can be invaluable for you to keep a dream journal in which you record and date your dreams. This way, you can observe when a particular theme appears and which situation in your life it coincides with. Many recurring dreams start promptly when a difficult situation starts and end when we extricate ourselves from that situation.

RESPONDING TO WARNING DREAMS

It is not necessary to respond to a warning dream with instant heroic action, but it is vital that you take it seriously. Particularly if a dream recurs, it is likely that something you have overlooked, endured, or rationalized in your personal life is actually harming you, at least emotionally. Any relationship can go through a period of crisis, and you may have dreams that are shocking at such junctures. If your relationship is stable, nourishing, and good for you, then deal with a period of difficulty by looking at the bigger picture. However, the warning dreams we have explored in this chapter are not typical of a rough patch in an otherwise-fine relationship—they are signals of a costly crisis that has the potential to rob dreamers of the enjoyment of their personal life. Never be afraid to take the messages of your heart seriously, and trust your own assessment of the situation.

Chapter 9

RELATIONSHIP DREAM
THEMES AND SYMBOLS

When it comes to matters of the heart, your dreams are focused on what will or will not make you happy. Love, attraction, and what you want all jostle for time onstage in your thoughts. This sets you up for confusion as you try to sort through what you want and how you feel, and you perhaps begin to second-guess yourself. We all know what it is like to be mesmerized by attraction, captivated by the lifestyle someone enjoys, or even electrified by the spark of desire. Your dreaming mind, though, could not care less about the way someone looks in tight blue jeans or the naughty, crooked smile that tugs at your heart. Your subconscious mind focuses on your happiness and well-being like a wise, loving grandmother. This part of your psyche is always trying to process answers to important questions such as the following:

· Will this person make you happy?
· Can this person commit for the long haul?
· Are you truly compatible, as friends and allies, as well as lovers?
· Will this person be good to and for your family?

- Do you feel better, stronger, and more comfortable with this person in your life?
- Do you have a high-quality love for each other?

Although you may find it hard to sort out all the variables that a new relationship presents, your subconscious is tracking the answers to those questions and running through them in your dreams. You certainly do not have to make important life decisions solely on the basis of your dreams, but it is smart to respect the way that your dreams are focused on and grounded in your ultimate happiness. By watching the course your dreams take, you will get an extremely accurate and early take on what lies beneath the surface of any new relationship.

Your dreams can be an invaluable source of insight and healing, but only if you think carefully about them. Let's explore some of the most common ways that relationship themes appear in modern dreams.

PICKING OUT A PUPPY

In this dream, you are picking out a puppy from a wide variety of possible pets. You want to get just the right one—the puppy that captures your heart, makes immediate eye contact with you, is quickly affectionate, and comes over to you as if it has been waiting just for you. You think you have found just the one. It is not the most beautiful, but it is cute in a homely way, with a lot of character and personality. It is impossible to tell what the puppy will look like when it grows up, but you feel an immediate pull—this puppy is meant for you.

This dream is a common one, particularly for young women from the late teen years through the midthirties. It is typically the dream of a woman who has not yet married but who is preparing her heart to make a commitment when she finds the right potential partner. The dream of selecting a puppy occurs when she meets someone who is "a possible" in her mind. In the symbolic language of dreams, dogs are sometimes associated with male energy, and certainly with love and loyalty. When women dream of selecting a dog or puppy, they are most often considering taking on a new romantic relationship. The puppy symbolizes a new relationship that has promise and excitement, which makes your heart melt. Yet it also represents a relationship that is new, because it is impossible to tell what it will become when it is more mature.

If you dream of picking out a puppy, you can assume that you are making space in your world for the possibility of a partner relationship and that you are going through a number of internal tasks in preparation for this. You are probably clearing away some of the clutter in your mind, heart, and lifestyle, which can only be good for you. You may be evaluating which qualities are most important to you in a mate.

You may notice you have the puppy dream more than once. This is a natural process and a good sign that you are involved in psychological, emotional, and perhaps even spiritual preparation. We have been taught, to some extent, that love is an accident, but being ready for love is not. All the preparation work you do is to your advantage. Being prepared for love allows you to be fully conscious of your experience, to avoid projecting old troubles onto a new partner, and to be confident in your instincts.

It's important to note that if you are planning on getting a new pet, then, of course, the interpretation of this dream is more literal. We do sometimes rehearse and explore such a wonderful addition in our dreams.

Going Fishing

In this dream, you are fishing in a stream that has a lot of interesting fish visible beneath the surface. You are interested in getting one particular fish rather than reeling in a vast number of them. You become very focused as you get what feels like a nibble, and then feel quite excited as there is a definite tug on your line. You begin to pull and then remember the proper technique for getting the fish out of the water. As you reel in the line, you see the fish you have caught and look at it eagerly to see if it is the one you have been trying to catch.

This dream is slightly more common among men who are searching for a woman, but a surprising number of women report the fishing dream, too, when they are in the process of screening potential partners. This is a dream that seems to occur most often when a promising potential lover has come on the scene. The dreamer is trying to see whether that person is indeed interested in her and whether she can captivate him sufficiently to begin a relationship. The dream seems to hint at some potential for manipulation, because the dreamer is dangling bait, waiting to hook prey, and then reeling it in. But I have not observed this to be a prominent motivation in the behavior or the emotional process of the dreamers who have shared this theme. Instead, the dream appears to present a metaphor for trying to single out a desired creature from its surroundings and to bring it forward for closer inspection.

Presumably, if the person under consideration does not prove an appropriate candidate, the dreamer will throw him back into the stream. In casual terms, I have overheard women talk to one another about "throwing that one back" when someone has proved unsuitable. There is also, of course, the very old saying (intended as consolation to disappointment) that there are plenty of fish in the sea.

If you have the fishing dream, you can assume that you are evaluating someone as a potential partner: that person's availability and interest in you, and appropriateness for you. Do not be disturbed by the apparent calculation or predatory inference in the dream metaphor. Because women are so vulnerable to love and sometimes to exploitation, women can be impressively flinty about screening out the bottom feeders. We tend to be so nonjudgmental with family, friends, and lovers that it is a good thing to be cautious and selective in the early scrutiny of a potential mate.

SENSUAL KISSING

In this dream, you are with someone you have recently met or someone who is a composite figure: part movie star and part attractive fictional character. He sidles up for an embrace and you turn to him, hesitating only a fraction of a second. Your lips are tantalizingly close, and then they meet. Your mind takes a vacation, as this is the sweetest, most soulful kiss in history.

Kissing someone in a dream allows you to try on a moment of sensuality and intimacy and sample what it might be like. Typically, women who have sensual kissing scenes in dreams have someone special in mind that they are trying to understand and evaluate as a love interest. In the early stages of a romance, we kiss to test the waters, to see what kind of chemistry rises up. Many women believe that as a man kisses, so he behaves as a lover. According to this theory, you can tell by kissing whether the other person is going to gobble at you like a dog eating ice cream or whether you will be elevated to ecstasy by the kiss. Whether or not this theory is true, in our dreams, we tend to have powerful feelings in response to kissing. We are either repelled or transported.

If you have a dream of sensual kissing, pay attention to how you felt and how the rest of the dream scenes unfolded. Perhaps the kissing was sensual and exciting but some difficulty followed that scene. It is no simple task to find someone who fulfills your needs to feel sensual and transported but is also a reliable and trustworthy partner. Although kissing dreams tend to assess sexual compatibility, they may also illustrate a challenge associated with a particular person. If you encounter a disaster after the kissing, such as rough treatment, ridicule, or a threat—or if you are hurt, abandoned or lost—the dream may provide a warning of hidden threats. If the dream was entirely pleasant, and you felt uplifted and stirred by it, then the implication is a positive one.

Sometimes kisses are featured in dreams that do not seem sensual, and the kiss itself is not erotic in nature. Sandi dreamed she was standing with her new male friend in front of a display of artwork at the local library. They simply stood enjoying the pictures, and then he turned and kissed her briefly, firmly, in a way that was sweet but not erotic. When we discussed the dream, she felt that the kiss was like a pact of understanding between them. He was someone who shared her enthusiasm for the arts and who appreciated and seemed to respect her own artistic endeavors. This dream kiss was a clue to her that, in that respect, her new association promised a level of understanding and mutual interest that she had always longed for.

If you dream of being kissed in a way that simply isn't sexy or of being kissed by someone whom you could never consider in a sexual way, it is possible that those dream kisses are not about sensual chemistry. Kisses in ancient times were considered a sign of recognition and appreciation. Sometimes dream kisses suggest the person who kisses you understands what you are all about and admires you. If a fictional character kisses you, it implies that you are recognizing yourself for following through, keeping a promise to yourself. You have been loyal to something important, and you have accomplished your mission. When you receive this kind of blessing kiss, your psyche is saying, "Well done!"

HEROIC FRIENDS

In this dream, you are involved in a grand adventure, an Indiana Jones–type of movie. You scale mountains, swing on vines, race around after treasures, and experience tension as well as the euphoria of sheer adrenaline. Your companion on the adventure is a fictional character, but one you know well in the dream. You are beyond friends and beyond lovers. This is a bond that cannot be broken. As you attempt to climb upward, you slip and cannot get your footing. Your companion warns you not to look down. You are not sure if you can manage this last portion of the journey, but just then, you feel his hands placing your foot into a toehold, and step-by-step, he guides you upward to safety and to victory. When you awaken from the dream, you may feel a surge of disbelief that this heroic man who was partner, friend, guide, and lifesaver does not actually exist in your waking life.

This theme can present itself in a variety of adventure settings, so you may recognize the underlying story more than the setting from your own dream. Essentially, there is high adventure, a quest, challenges, and a tremendous bond of camaraderie with someone who fights and struggles by your side. Together, you prevail against all odds; you take turns rescuing and helping each other to succeed.

The theme of high adventure with a heroic companion is often a signal of psychic preparation for a loving partnership. It sometimes occurs when someone you consider merely a friend is actually a suitable and devoutly loyal partner for you. This stirring adventure seems to be a reminder that life is an epic adventure: we all try to avoid the snake pits, and we all try to find our treasure. The comrade depicted in the dream is someone who stands by your side, laying down his life if need be, and helping you to walk on your path safely and successfully. As often occurs in dreams, this theme reminds us of the big picture, showing that life partners must be courageous and steadfast and that you both should remember to enjoy the grand adventure of life itself.

Some women have had a heroic-friends dream shortly before they met their significant other. Some had this dream and became open to a romance with someone who had long been a buddy but whose deep devotion they had not previously recognized and valued. In other cases, the dream served as a reminder that true connection, like a true calling, is not extinguished or lost, even though we are unable to control the timing of its presentation as much as we might wish. The invigorating implication of this dream is that you should not give up hope for a wonderful partner, and you should tackle your life with renewed vigor.

THE PRINCE AND THE PALACE

In this dream, a prince or tribal chief has chosen you to be the bride of one of the royal family. Although you wish you had time to lose a few pounds or get your legs waxed, you are whisked off and settled into a room in the palace to await the wedding preparations. You have mixed feelings about this. It's awfully satisfying to be selected to become one of the royal family, and the prince is attractive and attentive, but the way everyone is going about things seems a little rigid and old-fashioned. You meet with the prince, and he assures you that this is all meant to be. You begin to feel more comfortable with your fate, although secretly you are not sure why they chose you.

This is a dream that occurs when a relationship is showing the promise of eventual commitment. It is interesting that, in most cases, the theme includes a layer of ambivalence. We are accustomed to the fairy tales in which everything unfolds like a fantasy, but these dreams include a sense of bewilderment, a worry that the new regime may be restricting, and concern that becoming part of the royal family (a traditional marriage) may lead to reduced personal freedom.

If you experience this dream theme, you may be trying to sort through the implications of your current relationship and decide in advance how you will respond if he proposes. The dream does not typically give you an answer; instead, it gives you a way to cut to the bottom line and process the major considerations. Do you want to become part of this person's extended family? Do you feel comfortable with the rules and expectations this person brings along (life in the palace)? Do you understand why this person loves you or is set on you? In some versions of this dream, the woman bears many scars on her body, and she dreads the wedding night, when the prince will see her and find her disfigured. The implication is that she worries about past wounds from prior relationships and how they may affect her ability to be close and to trust in this relationship.

If you recognize this theme, it is time for you to take stock. If you have been holding intimacy at bay, trying to sort everything out on your own, it may be time to have a talk with your partner and see what kind of space there is to explore mutual fears and hopes. This should not turn into an ultimatum, a threat, or a demand for commitment. Rather, at a time that feels suitable and safe, make time to talk gently about the hopes and worries you each may be experiencing.

When this dream presents itself without a real-life relationship in the background, you can presume that you are exploring a different sort of promise in your life. You may be launching a business, writing your first book, or taking your paintings to your first exhibit. There is something big and slightly scary going on that brings with it significant promise, and deeply personal fears. If this makes sense to you, then your task is to be brave, to fulfill your promise as best you can, and to be gentle with the part of you that feels exposed or fearful.

RECOVERY OR RENEWAL

In dreams of recovery or renewal, you discover that you simply misplaced a beloved object you thought you had lost. This is so exciting that it's better than getting something brand new. You clean it off and feel a rush of happy memories and delight that you had not lost it after all. It was here the whole time!

In some versions of this dream, you discover that a pet or a plant you thought was dead has magically sprung back to life. The cat, once dead, is dancing to a song on the radio, suddenly very much alive! Or the flowers that had run out of water now blossom as if by magic.

These dreams of restoration and recovery often come at times when we are finding a deep kind of happiness, the kind that comes when we embrace our own qualities and feel connected with others and with life. Falling in love restores us and gives us permission to be happy and content in a profound way. If you notice dreams of restoration as you enter a love relationship, they are a wonderful signal from your subconscious that your present love is helping you heal and recover parts of yourself that you may have thought you'd lost. You can help this process along by giving yourself special permission to tackle the things that have been on your "to-do someday" list: such as joining the gym, rearranging your living room, or even tracking down your childhood best friend. This is a time of inspiration and renewal, so make good use of it.

MAGNIFICENT WILD ANIMALS

A stunning creature, such as a lioness, an elephant, a wild stallion, or a whale, befriends you in a dream. Although you are a little nervous at first, it quickly becomes apparent that the creature does not mean you harm and in fact is prepared to give you safe passage out of the forest or across the tundra or back to shore. As you travel with it, you may communicate telepathically with the animal or at least feel that you have a strong rapport and understanding. This sense of magical connection stays with you when you awaken, and you may feel a little shaken and moved throughout the day as a result.

The extraordinary wild animals in our dreams typically represent our own powers as a person. The friendship of a wild animal can often reflect a reconnection with your own power, authority, and courage. The kindling of a romance or the solidity of a loving partnership grants us access to the wealth of power we have always had but may not feel on a daily basis. This walk with the wild, powerful creatures of nature reflects a renewed sense of your own authority and strength as an individual.

If you have had such a dream, then do not underestimate your abilities to lead, to take charge, or to succeed at something daring.

This is a time when you are connected with and in possession of your special powers! This is a wonderful comment on your current relationship or the one you are starting.

TOILETS

In this dream, you are searching for a toilet and finding it strangely difficult. You experience a number of dead-ends and disappointments but then finally locate a public restroom. Unfortunately, once you get there, it is not in good repair or is terribly dirty with overflowing commodes. You simply can't use the restroom, and you leave, but the situation is becoming more urgent and you're going to have to do something.

This dream reflects a need to have an outlet for your own expression, to let down your hair, or to unburden yourself emotionally. This dream is typical of people who act as the informal therapist for others but never get to talk about their own problems. It is also the dream of frustrated artists or writers who are overflowing with ideas and have so many inspirations on hold that they are starting to feel overwhelmed.

If you notice this type of theme in your dreams as you begin a relationship or as your relationship solidifies, consider whether you have been dismissing your own needs for the demands of others. You are probably a natural giver and a naturally healing personality, but you have to take care of yourself, your feelings, your ideas, and your inspirations as well. Even a minor change in the way you manage your time or prioritize your needs can make a huge difference in how you feel and what you accomplish. Your relationship may be a great one, but it will become even better and more solid when you make sure that you have an outlet for your expression and a sounding board for your ideas.

Swimming Joyously

Regardless of whether you like water or know how to swim in waking life, in this dream, you swim effortlessly, with great joy and abandon. You can dive into beautiful water and swim like an Olympic star or a mermaid. The process is sensual, exciting, and delicious, particularly if you have not done it before. If you do not swim in real life, you may even wonder at the ease of the process and feel surprise and delight that you have discovered something so rewarding and fun.

In our dreams, swimming is often symbolic of emotional freedom and fluency, of the ability to communicate, connect, and exchange with others in an environment that is welcoming and safe. This is a typical dream to have in a relationship that affords you a new freedom to be yourself, to feel safe and celebrated by another. It is common to have a dream of delightful swimming or even swimming lessons when you enter a relationship that takes you to a new level of intimacy and confidence.

If you have a dream of joyous swimming, view it symbolically as a celebration of your emotional freedom and your confidence that the real you is safe to come out and play, sure to be loved and appreciated in a way that you may not know. The water in this dream is like a warm emotional environment in which you can stay afloat and navigate easily; you have emotionally come home.

Shopping and Buying New Outfits

In this dream, you are at the mall or your favorite shopping territory, surveying some desirable choices and trying on clothes. You have some pretty specific ideas about what you are looking for, and you discard a lot of things that are nice but not quite right. Despite the variety of choices, you are not discouraged and feel confident about finding the right items.

Shopping in dreams is comparable to making choices in life. You are sorting through options and determining what suits you, what works for you, and what will make you happy. There are times when you have to be extremely specific about what you want and decide not to let other choices distract you. There are also times when you are in the groove and find tons of things that are simply perfect for you. Shopping dreams are often celebrations of your power to choose and to move on to a new phase in life. It is normal to have shopping dreams when you are entering a new relationship or when the relationship you're in is becoming serious, and you are both ready for a commitment. If the shopping expedition in your dream is frustrating and unsuccessful, you may not understand your current situation and need more time to get clear before you can make satisfying and decisive choices.

In general, if you are successful and on track with your shopping dream, you can feel confident in your current decisions and instincts. If the shopping dream is frustrating and anxiety producing, then adopt a strategy of patience and watchfulness, giving yourself time to sort things out to your satisfaction before making a big decision.

COMING HOME

In this dream, you have returned home to the place you grew up or the location that you consider your emotional home. Things are essentially as you remember them, but you feel a new emotional confidence and freedom. The minor things that used to bug you now seem charming and harmless, and you feel connected with your old friends and even your old enemies in a way that makes you feel whole, grown up, secure, and happy.

The dream of coming home and seeing that place through genuinely loving eyes is something that may happen at any time of life when you have moved into a phase of personal power, maturity, and love. It is particularly common to have dreams with this theme when you are successfully in love or have been enriched by seeing yourself reflected in the love of your partner. The home in the dream suggests that you have found your emotional home in your love relationship; it implies that the presence of a deep and authentic romance is renewing and healing your entire life and history. We truly can be healed and restored in the present in a way that washes away friction and fear from the past.

If you have had a dream of a benevolent homecoming, then you are almost certainly experiencing a personal emotional victory—whether you are preparing for love, exploring a new connection, or celebrating the love you have. Don't be surprised if you feel as though someone has taken out your insides, washed and fluffed them, and put them back in again, making you feel new inside and out. This is not the temporary euphoria of infatuation but the genuine transformation of mature love.

FLASHBACK DREAMS

In the flashback dream, you are back in an old relationship with someone you have not seen in years. You are surprised to find yourself back in this relationship, and you mentally scramble to try to figure out what this means to your present and future. How will this arrangement work? Where will you live? Will the old problems continue to be a challenge? How could you have renewed this relationship, without really noticing what was happening?

Relationship flashback dreams are perhaps the most common of all romantic themes, and although we have touched on this theme already, it is very important to understand. In positive versions of this dream, you realize suddenly that this person from the past is the one great love of your life and that, now that you have gotten together once more, your life is actually beginning again. Although it may be tempting to view this theme literally and try to get in touch with your old flame when you wake up with your heart thumping, it is far more likely that this dream reflects a positive connection with some new person in your life. In the symbolic language of dreams, your mind is saying, "Ah, I see you have found the real thing. Now you can begin to spread your wings and enjoy an authentic, rewarding love in your life."

If you have had this type of dream, consider the qualities that make a relationship work for you and the way your heart and your nature respond to the person in your life now. Although that person may be entirely different from your old flame, when we encounter a love that is wholesome and that suits us to the very core, the mind attempts to express this good fit by using symbols from your history. This is time to give the relationship you have a certain chance to blossom and assume a higher priority in your life.

However, some more negative versions of this dream are like a romantic nightmare in which you are back with someone you wouldn't want. This dream is a warning not to be drawn into an arrangement that is unfair to you; not to fall for whatever your weakness may be; and most important, not to conduct yourself in a way that you have already outgrown personally, emotionally, and spiritually. If you wake up to this pattern in your life, you can certainly dismiss it. As with all dream insights, if you are willing to see what is true for you, then you can trust yourself to know what decisions, if any, you need to make.

THUMBS-UP, THUMBS-DOWN

In this dream, you are with someone you recognize as a new person in your life. You are on a date, away for a weekend, or spending a romantic evening at home cuddling. The plot may take a turn toward the bizarre as things grow more passionate or intimate. Your companion reveals he is actually an alien from Pluto or that he is half man, half lizard. You suddenly think this is not such a great bargain for you and make polite excuses to end the evening early.

In more positive versions of this dream, you find that your companion suits you wonderfully. You may or may not make love, but the sense of connection and ease with one another is palpable, exciting, and satisfying.

It is typical in these dreams that your companion does not look like the new person in your life. There may be some exaggerated physical characteristic that is similar, such as size, hairstyle, manner, or eye color, but often the appearance is altogether different. Do not be confused by this; notice the qualities of your dream companion instead.

If you have a dream like this shortly after dating a new person, then view the dream as giving you a first impression from your deeper mind. Often the dream takes a dramatically positive or negative view of the new person, showing you an absurd (but often apt) mismatch. If things are more positive, the dream gives the new person in your life a rave review. Use this dream as an advantageous bit of inside information, not a demand that you either terminate or pursue the connection.

THE FACELESS GROOM

You are getting married! You are at the church and everyone is there. The music is playing and your gown is perfect. You walk down the aisle and reach the altar. Your fiancé meets you and you join hands, gazing at each other. At this point, you notice that your fiancé has no face. There is just a shadow there or a blank space where his face should be. This doesn't bother you in the dream, however, and the ceremony continues. When you awaken, you cannot help but wonder why you were marrying a faceless guy and why this didn't strike you as even remotely odd.

This is a dream that many women report, particularly women younger than thirty. It is a dream that women seem to have before they have been married, when they are wondering who will come along and what their future holds. In one sense, the dream is a rehearsal, but long before the partner has arrived on the scene. Dreams are to some extent developmental; that is, we dream of big events and new chapters in life before we undertake them. In this way, we explore what the change will be like, and we prepare mentally and emotionally for what lies ahead.

If you have this type of dream, you may be exploring the type of partner you want and what your wedding might be like. There is nothing wrong with considering your preferences before you meet the right guy. If a wedding is part of what you look forward to, with all its celebration and shared experience, then exploring it in your dreams is one way to separate the personal bits from the traditional elements. Should you meet someone special, be careful not to cast that person as simply part of your personal movie. You may find him to be perfect for the role you have in mind, but never forget to accept him as an individual who is very real in his own right.

WEDDING DISASTERS

In this dream, you are getting married to your fiancé when something goes terribly wrong. The caterer does not arrive or brings live eels instead of the cake you ordered. Your dress is hideously flawed, or your groom shows up and reveals himself to be a troglodyte or a Frankenstein monster in a tuxedo. You are brokenhearted and embarrassed—there is no way to hide this disaster from public view, and all the people who matter most to you are there to witness your personal trauma. While we may dream of weddings in general as we explore what and whom we want, wedding disaster themes tend to be the anxiety dreams of women who are engaged.

If you are in fact planning your wedding, then don't freak out if you have a few nightmares about weddings gone awry. The pressures of a wedding are significant, and they can put the bride smack between a rock and a hard place. There are social and familial expectations, religious traditions, contrasts between the preference and style of the bride's family and the groom's family, as well as the way the couple hopes that their friends view and witness the wedding. In addition, there are the individual concerns and fantasies of the couple themselves. Sometimes it seems there is no room left for the couple to enjoy and stand in the spotlight of their commitment and promise to each other, because they are suddenly starring in a drama created by the expectations of others.

The bride, who may have the highest expectations of all and to whom the ritual may mean the most, often feels she has the least say in the proceedings and that she cannot let down others who are sidling for control. If you add to this mix the fact that the bride is going through a psychological and emotional initiation, with all the accompanying internal shifts and upheavals, the tension can be quite high. One way to explore this tension is to race through nightmare scenarios in which all is lost and disaster strikes. Although these dreams do not seem to be helpful at the time, they in fact help you to explore worries and process bottled-up anxiety.

If you have wedding nightmares, then it is a great time to talk with friends who are married and hear about their accounts of similar dreams. This is a natural part of processing the tension associated with weddings, and these dreams are extremely common. In general, the worry is focused on letting down others and their expectations, being seen publicly in a foolish light, or discovering something dreadful about your fiancé. If you are able to see which element in the dream is the most fearful, you may understand something specific about what tension is eating at you. Your task is to try to pace yourself. Make sure you have time to think out loud with trusted friends and have down time with your fiancé. Treat yourself with kindness, and be very gentle if you start to feel unraveled. You will get through this, enjoy your day, and find that your fiancé is not a troglodyte.

THE UNSUITABLE GIFT

In this dream, you have received a gift from you partner, maybe a ring or another rather large present. Everyone congratulates you, and you feel yourself being swept away on a journey toward marriage. Although you are proud and excited, there is something unusual about the gift that you do not understand. When you are alone, you realize that the gift is something that is not your style or something that other people tend to value but you do not. You feel a little tense, because your acceptance of the gift has been construed as the acceptance of a proposal. You feel you need time to understand what this means. It is not a gift that is right for you! It remains to be seen whether the gift was an insignificant error on the part of your lover or whether it implies that he is not seeing and knowing you for who you truly are.

This theme is rather unsettling for the people who experience it. One of the challenges most romantic partners face is the human tendency to give something we ourselves value instead of giving what the other person would value. The gift in the dream likely has little to do with actual presents and is more symbolic of how your partner treats you and shows you affection. So, the woman in love with a scuba diver might receive a harpoon in her dream when she would much prefer a piece of jewelry or a new kitten. There is a peculiar loneliness that envelops us when we feel that the person most important to us is apparently blind to our unique traits and doesn't seem to know the first thing about us. This dream is not necessarily a bad omen about your relationship, but it does hint that you are not feeling the other person sees you as well as you would like.

This may be a time to schedule some activity or time together in which you can become better acquainted and let yourself be known. This is a dream that often occurs after the initial phase of a relationship when you have passed all the hurdles and are beginning to determine whether you have a future together. During the early phase, when the relationship is in the screening process, both people behave as if they are on a job interview: they present themselves in their most charming and attractive light, hoping they will be acceptable to the other person, whom they are falling for. Once you pass this phase, there can be a jolt of uneasiness if you realize that you may be in love with someone who has little idea who you really are. All of a sudden, the edited version of yourself is not serving your happiness at all! It hurts when your partner relates to an image of you instead of the real you.

Don't despair. This dream likely is helping you transition from the audition phase to the connecting phase of your romance. (But if there is something seriously wrong with the relationship, you will likely have a rapid succession of dreams in which you are not seen or in which you are treated in a way that wounds you.) A single presentation of the inappropriate-gift theme provides you with a chance to let yourself become better acquainted with your love and provides both of you with the chance to grant each other permission to share and explore each other in a safe harbor of acceptance.

INTERRUPTED INTIMACY

You are with your partner in a romantic situation and leading up to lovemaking. Just as things are getting interesting, someone unexpected interrupts you. It may be one of your parents or a mutual friend or even an ex-lover. The interrupting party asks a simple question, like, "Where is the mustard?" while the two of you are frozen in place. You know this is off the wall, but the interrupting person seems to have no clue there is anything unusual or awkward going on.

This is a dream that both men and women experience, although it seems more common among women, and women seem to find it more troubling. The interruption symbolizes an influence or a situation in your waking life that is inhibiting your ability to enjoy your relationship as fully as you would like. Although the dream places the situation squarely in your sex life, the implication of the dream is broader; it refers to your relationship itself and all the levels of intimacy that outside influences have dimmed.

You may be able to deduce the situation that is intruding into your private space by identifying the interrupting person. If it is a family member or a parent, then family responsibilities, traditions, or mythology may be intruding into your relationship. If it is your boss or a work associate, your work may be pressing in on your private time. An intrusion by an old flame, either yours or your lover's, suggests that some feelings from the past are intruding into the present intimacy.

Cindy, a new bride, reported having a dream that her mother-in-law was with her and her husband in their bedroom, making helpful suggestions on how to take good care of her son. Although superficially revolting and disturbing, the dream's imagery underscored the bride's sense that she was being measured against an invisible standard, not sexually, but emotionally, and this was shaking her confidence. She took the opportunity to discuss the situation with her husband, who fortunately was neither upset nor surprised by her feelings, and they made a pact to present a stronger alliance to everyone in their lives, making it clear that they were a team and that they loved their relatives but their relatives were not on the team.

We all experience times when our relationship is heaven and other times when we are trying hard but not feeling quite right. The dream of interrupted intimacy is a signal that it is time to orient to the situation in a somewhat different way. You will know if your partner will receive a frank discussion well, and if you focus on revealing rather than blaming, then it certainly should be frank. This is a time when you want and need emotional boundaries to be strengthened so that you can feel that what you share together is sacred territory where others do not trespass. Whether the intrusion is related to work, friends, kids, or relatives, make a pact that you will both make it a priority to keep this part of your lives special, separate, and free from worries.

MULTIPLE PARTNERS SHOW UP

You're off on a mini-vacation with your partner and arrive at the hotel feeling happy and anticipating a good time. As you arrive, you see that your former boyfriend is there, too, waiting in the lobby and reading a magazine. In a flash, you remember that you promised to meet him there, as well, for a romantic weekend together. What on earth were you thinking? Why would you do that? Now what are you going to do? You desperately try to steer your partner in a different direction so that he doesn't spot your old boyfriend sitting there waiting for you. This is a mess. Your mind goes a hundred miles an hour as you try to sort out how this is going to work.

The details and setting of this dream differ, but it is a common dream for women to have at the beginning or toward the end of a relationship. It also seems to occur when a current relationship is approaching the stage at which you feel you must either break up or get married.

The old lover represents a different scenario from the relationship of the present. He not only is someone you probably cared about but also symbolizes a different possible life for you. Early in a new relationship, the options all bounce around in your mind, and it is still unclear which way is the right path. Toward the end of a relationship, even if you have felt quite committed, it is as if new windows have opened in your mind, and you begin to see that your life could take quite a different turn if the relationship does draw to a close. At the crisis point of a relationship, when there is an invisible pressure to either commit or leave, you may also feel the presence of other choices and seem conflicted or confused about what you should do. It is not so much that you are trying to choose between one man and another; you are struggling to discern the best path for your life to take at this point.

Women have a fine-tuned sense of emotional faithfulness. Women may not always be faithful, but they do feel emotionally loyal to their partners. Entertaining other possibilities or corresponding with male friends or old boyfriends on the side may be technically harmless and not considered infidelity. But these activities can sometimes be the manifestation of a longing to consider other courses in life aside from that with a current partner. These scenarios can create a sense of guilt, as though you have been disloyal to your partner by letting yourself entertain other options. Allow yourself some guilt-free reflection to investigate what your feelings may truly be as you unravel the dream.

If you are going through a time of complicated assessments about what direction to take, determining whether and to whom you wish to commit, your first duty is to take care of yourself. Most women feel drained and fragmented when they are unsure of their relationships or unsure of their decisions. Don't spread yourself too thin or feel overly responsible for everyone around you. It may take some time before your preference and your best choices become clear to you, and you deserve to let the horizon come clear in your own mind. This is not a time to beat yourself up or to put undue pressure on your process. Be kind to others, and be kind to yourself.

HE IS UNFAITHFUL

In this dream, you discover that your lover or husband is being unfaithful. You catch him with the new girl at the office, or you discover him with some other woman who really is not his type. You are devastated but also bewildered. How could you not have known about this? How could he make such a weird selection if he wanted to cheat? You are furious and may even throw something at him before storming out.

Almost all women who have ever been married or in a

committed relationship have dreamed that their partner cheated on them. This dream occurs when your partner has shifted gears and is shining the spotlight of his attention somewhere else. Interestingly, this dream seldom occurs when someone is actually cheating. That is the good news! It seems to symbolize the pain you feel when someone who used to shower you with attention is more interested in going fishing with his friends or working overtime on a regular basis. Women also have this dream when their partner gets a new toy, such as a motorcycle, which may feel for a while like he has found a new passion and it isn't you! Anything that makes you feel like you are not number one anymore can stimulate the dream of infidelity.

If you have this dream, it is a great idea to share the scenario with your partner and to let him know you are feeling like you have moved out of his spotlight. Explain that you do not mind his enthusiasm for his hobby (or whatever it may be), but that you need some quality time together to feel close again. Never underestimate the power of stating what you need and what you both should do to correct the situation. You may be upset because the dream illustrates the very real hurt you have been experiencing unconsciously for some time. Also, the visual memory of seeing your partner in someone else's arms can shake you up badly.

Try to communicate your needs and feelings without blaming or attacking your partner. After all, he hasn't actually done anything wrong, and he may not understand how you could be so upset with him because of a dream. This confrontation can be pretty strange for him, coming (as he sees it) from out of nowhere. He will understand when you say that dreams of infidelity are about feeling second best and that you want to feel like number one again. Help him understand that he needs to take some action to repair things, and give him concrete suggestions on how he can show you that you are number one. He will probably realize instinctively that he has entered a danger zone. Don't insist that he comprehend all the nuances of your dream and the psychological implications. Just get him on board with a concrete plan of action, and the improved emotional climate should take its course.

You Are Unfaithful

In this dream, you are having a great time with an impulsive fling. You may have met an old flame you never could resist or just got carried away while on a business trip or while visiting family. Oops! Although you had a good time, you really are not a cheater and you break out in a cold sweat when the fling is over. What on earth were you thinking? What are you going to tell your partner if he finds out? He can't find out. Your mind darts around as you try to figure out whether he will, in fact, find out what you have done. Will he leave you? Probably. How could you have been so careless?

This is a dream more common among women in their twenties and early thirties. Typically, the dreamers have not had an affair at all, but there is something that is nagging at their conscience. This dream may present in a brief series, say, two or three times, until you wonder why you are always dreaming of cheating when that is not your style. You might think about cheating, but you wouldn't actually do it, even if you felt like it, because it seems disrespectful or disloyal.

This dream is amplifying some feeling you have that you are committing an act of disloyalty. The general theme is that of betraying someone (or something) you care about, not deliberately, but unthinkingly. Out of necessity, many women have contingency plans in the back of their minds. If something happens to this relationship, where will you go next? Would you move back to your hometown? Would you apply for that job overseas? Would you go back to your old flame, the guy who proposes to you four times a year? Sometimes these dreams of cheating occur when we are going over our contingency plans or when we take actions to keep them viable.

If this makes sense to you, then it is likely that something you're exploring on your own is making you feel a little guilty toward your partner. This doesn't necessarily mean that you are doing the wrong thing. If you are contemplating a contingency plan because you are not sure how the relationship is going to go, then you are certainly within your rights to do so, particularly if you have small children or other responsibilities you have to prioritize.

Sometimes people do conduct flirtations or platonic affairs and consider these okay because there is no sex involved. It is up to you to decide whether these are indeed okay for you and whether you would feel all right about it if the tables were turned.

Dana had been in a relationship for several years. When it ended, she quickly began dating someone new. For months afterward, she had dreams that she was cheating on her former partner. Although the relationship was over, she still felt loyal and emotionally responsible for her former companion. With time, these dreams and the feelings that formed them faded away. It is up to you to evaluate whether you are doing or contemplating anything about which you should feel guilty. Don't judge yourself harshly or create drama where there is none. Do no harm, and let your brilliant sanity be your guide.

TRAVELING TOGETHER IN A CAR

You are with your partner, traveling by car. You are not clear on the destination, but your partner seems to know where you are going. There is something weird about the situation, but you can't quite place your finger on it. The car you are in may or may not be your actual car. It is only when you awaken that you can recall what it was that seemed strange about the dream.

There are varieties of themes involving traveling with your loved one in a car. These different themes are associated with different meanings. The following are broad suggestions based on other dreamers' experiences, but they are a good place to start examining your own dream scenario.

BRIDGE TROUBLE

In this theme, you are traveling across a large bridge when some difficulty arises. The bridge may be out halfway through, or there may be a wreck on the bridge that serves to block and back up traffic. You may have car trouble that makes it necessary for you to get out of the car and proceed on foot across the bridge. You may look off into the distance and notice that you have taken the wrong freeway somehow and that you want to be "over there" somewhere. This is frustrating, because you can't get there from where you are.

Bridges often symbolize the methods we use to try to connect two things that seem separate. Just as a bridge spans empty space so we can travel from point A to point B, so our behaviors in a relationship attempt to connect us to the other person. We want to blend our families, we need to coordinate our career plans, and we strive to make room for mutual beliefs and faiths so we can have a life together. When you dream of encountering trouble on a bridge and your partner is with you, this suggests some trouble with the attempts to connect your two lives together. Consider whether your overall plan makes sense or whether it is time to discuss a different approach to the logistical and emotional connections you have both been trying to forge.

PECULIAR DRIVING SITUATIONS

You may find yourself taking a backseat while your partner drives your car. When you wake up, you wonder, "Why did I stay in the backseat like that?" In dreams, whoever is driving the car may be the person who is currently driving the relationship itself. Some women dream that they are in the backseat together with their partner while someone quite different drives the car. Whoever is driving the car may well be the person who is unofficially dominating the relationship or the family situation at that time. Sometimes this symbolic driver is an in-law, parent, deceased spouse, stepchild, or someone's boss.

While we are all so busy trying to get everything done and keep the peace, it is easy to miss the fact that someone inappropriate has begun to dominate the situation and to have undue influence on the family or a relationship. Dreams like this put you on notice that you don't want to sit back while someone else drives your life. There is no need to be hostile or to overreact, but it is a good idea to reassert your authority over your own experience on a variety of levels.

NO ONE IS DRIVING THE CAR

In this dream, you are traveling along looking out the window. You and your partner may be chatting comfortably, but at some point, you feel a wave of uneasiness followed swiftly by panic. It has dawned on you that no one is driving the car. You wiggle desperately into the driver's seat and try to take control. Each of you had assumed the other was driving, and it took quite a while for you to see that you were racing along the freeway full speed ahead with no one at the wheel.

This dream suggests that both of you are striving to do what the other one prefers, but nobody is really tracking the overall direction of the relationship. This is an excellent time to sit down and find out what your partner is thinking. Where does he want to live? Where does he see himself in five years? The dream does not depict either one of you wanting to bail out of the car (the relationship). Rather, it is a picture of incorrect assumptions and poor direction and planning. It is easy to think that you are taking a certain direction to please the other person, when the other person, in fact, is going along with what he believes to be your preference. Take some time to explore the default course you have both been on, and see if it makes sense or if there is another direction you have both been longing to take.

LOOKING BEHIND YOU

As you drive along, you are both looking in the rearview mirror. This seems fine, but after a while, you realize that you have neglected to look in front of you at all. You have spent all your time looking at the road behind you and truly have no sense of where you are going. Your partner has been doing the same thing. It is fortunate that you have been able to navigate with relative safety because you certainly have not paid the slightest attention to the road ahead.

This dream implies that you (and your partner) have for some reason allowed the past to dominate your thinking. You may be missing out on the present, as well as the future, because of a tendency to focus too much on the past. The dream makes a dramatic point: you would never attempt to move forward at high speed while looking backward. Don't attempt to live your life that way either! The past is always with us, and it should be, as rich experiences and a set of references upon which we can draw. But it should not be a map of our future.

Sometimes we become accustomed to reviewing past disasters in an attempt to steer away from similar pain in the future. In other cases, we idealize the past, behaving as if our happiness were lost in a mythical time capsule and good things were no longer available in the present and the future. In relationships, there is an unconscious tendency to attribute blame to one person or incident, and from there draw lines of cause and effect outward and onward indefinitely. Certainly the past contributes to present possibilities, but it need not continue to send pulsations into your present unless you resuscitate it on a daily basis. Honor the wisdom you have gained from your past, and release any emotional attachment (or drama) associated with it. This will let you orient to the future from a position of strength, wisdom, and solid confidence in your clarity.

A Cruise Together

In this dream, you are on a cruise with your partner. It is supposed to be a vacation, a time of intimacy, but there are strange happenings on the ship. You encounter a storm, or hostile creatures such as sharks may have surrounded the ship. The ship may spring a leak (like the *Titanic*), or there may be a fire onboard.

Themes of travel challenges typically occur at the midpoint of a relationship, when personality differences have begun to impede the flow of the relationship. The voyage represents the love affair; the difficulties represent the challenges you face. Storms are associated with emotion, predators may symbolize negativity or criticism, and fire and explosions may symbolize rage or explosive issues.

If you dream of a disastrous cruise together, you may be struggling with a collection of difficulties in the relationship that are all flaring up at once. This does not necessarily imply that the relationship is doomed, but many people have this dream when they have turned a corner and have begun to feel that they are in a situation that will not work for them. This is a time to examine your other dreams as well: if you are feeling hopeless, your dreams will reflect that feeling and present the same message in different ways. When an issue is boiling beneath the surface, you may notice dreams of crisis in a variety of plots: falling from a height, being unable to find what you are looking for in an emergency, lacking a private and clean restroom when you need it, or being unable to get the elevator to take you to the right floor. Even if the problem the dream depicts is rather silly, if it makes you feel panicky, frustrated, or overwhelmed in the dream, then the problem is a version of a crisis theme.

If you suspect that you have an emotional crisis catalyzed by circumstance, give yourself permission to gather impressions and listen to your deepest feelings. There is nothing to fear in recognizing what you already know on a deep level. Crisis dreams do not mean our problems are impossible to solve. Instead they often indicate that we don't own our feelings in some way, or that we are cutting off a portion of our experience because it is not aligned with how we believe we ought to feel.

Lana is a young mother who is able to stay home with her kids and who has a loving, faithful husband. She said that because she is wiped out from taking care of the kids, she finds her husband rather demanding sexually, and she sometimes resents his overtures at the end of a long day when she needs to get up early in the morning to tend to the little ones. She does not approve of her resentment about sex because she is grateful and loyal to her husband. She is tired, frayed at the edges sometimes, and wishes he would let her rest. Because she disapproves of her feelings of resentment, she dismisses them before she can really put a name to them. She recently dreamed that she and her husband were on a cruise together. She was carrying a child in each arm while he strode about the deck relaxing and grinning from ear to ear. She was annoyed that he did not offer to help her carry one of the kids but seemed to feel all was perfect in their world. In the same week, she dreamed that he had carelessly knocked down her fish tank, and she had found all her fish dried out, dead, and stuck to the floor. The cruise dream reflected the subject of her resentment, and the dream of the dead fish showed her that she was feeling burned out and lacking the refreshment and rest that would restore her interest and enthusiasm for romance. Because her dreams had shown her that the issue and her feelings were not going away on their own, she decided to offer her husband a deal of sorts, adjusting the childcare schedule and dividing some chores so that she could get some rest. In exchange, she promised him that she would not give him "the fish eye" when he expressed an interest in sex. So far, the pact has proven successful, and she is starting to feel like a lover again instead of an exhausted nanny.

PASSIONATE DANCING

In this dream, you are dancing with a partner in a wild, passionate style. You are able to dance as you always have longed to in your head—you can leap, bend, pound the floor with flamenco precision, and wrap yourself around your partner like a sinewy tango dancer.

Partner dancing symbolizes sexual and emotional chemistry. The passionate style of the dance is a promising signal that the fires of attraction and romantic love are well under way. This is a falling-in-love dream that most often occurs in the early stages of a relationship or just prior to starting a love affair. The implications of the dream are that you have indeed found someone who ignites passionate feelings and that the relationship will be a grand passion in your life.

If you have had this dream, you are probably at the point where there is no turning back from this relationship—nor would you want to! The dream does not offer information about compatibility or how enduring the relationship will be, however; it is a celebration dream, which typically occurs when there is a discovery of some significance and a promise of joy that is substantial.

BEING NAKED OR PARTLY DRESSED IN PUBLIC

In this dream, while out on a date with your loved one, you notice that you are only partially dressed. You forgot to put your pants on and you are downtown in your panties! Or you are wearing some shorts but you are topless. This is pretty confusing (how could you forget something like that?). You are also feeling a little vulnerable and exposed. You are not exactly embarrassed or ashamed, but you feel a little less comfortable than you would like to feel.

Our clothes in dreams tend to represent the different roles we have in our lives. Being underdressed or inappropriately dressed is a theme that frequently arises when we feel stressed, unprepared, or uncertain in a new role. Other people in the dreams do not seem to notice your predicament—the dream reflects how you feel. Although the dream suggests that you may feel vulnerable, other people do not pay much attention to your exposure.

Although you may have mastered a swift social transition from friendship to a full-blown love affair, there is often some natural emotional lag time involved. This is a dream that often happens during the stage of a relationship when you move from dating to intimacy. It takes time to get a feel for how you will be together and operate socially as a couple. All of these ambiguities will become clearer in time, but during the initial leap from friendship to love, you may feel nuances of uncertainty in your new role, particularly if you are a sensitive personality. This is a time to be gentle with yourself, and keep in mind that you may feel nervous or ambivalent about the expectations you face (such as meeting the family, attending office parties, introducing each other to friends). It is possible, even likely, that things will get a little shaky at times, even if your partner is a great person and you have a great new relationship. The swiftness with which we live our lives and make changes adds to the burden of all that we have to emotionally digest and master. You will grow into the social dimension of your relationship more easily if you make room for a variety of feelings and don't bludgeon yourself with the expectation of perfection.

CHANGES IN YOUR APPEARANCE

In this dream, you walk by a mirror or store window and notice a wonderful change in your appearance. Your hair may suddenly be flowing behind you in a long waterfall of luxurious waves. Your figure is exactly as you have always wanted it to be, and your clothes look terrific on you. Amazing that you had never realized before that you actually have a haunting kind of beauty. You are really, truly beautiful in your own way.

This is a dream (with myriad variations) that women report

when they are rediscovering themselves in a positive way. It occurs when something has given you a new lease on life. Noticing the positive change in your appearance represents a new kind of self-acceptance and joy in your uniqueness. For women, feeling beautiful and comfortable is more important than looking perfect. This is a dream of celebration and self-acceptance that often happens when you are starting a healthy relationship with someone who delights in your unique qualities.

If you dream of delighting in some facet of your appearance or of suddenly recognizing that you are beautiful, you are on the right track in your personal life. If you are not in a relationship at the time you have this dream, you are likely granting yourself permission to follow through on your goals and to explore your interests with enthusiasm. The basic message of this dream is true: you are unique and special, and the more you accept and delight in your qualities, the richer and more beautiful your life will become.

BEING RESCUED

In this dream, there is something after you—a snake, a giant spider, or even a serial killer. Like a heroine in a thriller, you maneuver to avoid the deadly threat, but each move you make seems to only postpone the inevitable. The scary thing is closing in on you, and the tension skitters through your body until you are on the verge of panic. Then your partner arrives and manages to save you! Your partner drives off the threat and then embraces you and comforts you. You can hardly believe the danger is over as you sink into his arms.

This dream often occurs early on in a relationship that has particularly solid footing. The scene suggests that the mutuality of your relationship will provide a safe haven, allowing you to finally put to rest some of the old demons of your past. The unconscious mind is not in the business of childish fantasies; rather, it tends to present the rescue theme when emotional healing is available.

The personal implication of this dream is not so much that your loved one will somehow save you from all your problems. We always ultimately rescue ourselves, but we are better able to do so when we open up to experience the love, support, and faith that others extend to us. This is a dream of affirmation that you have a window of opportunity available not only to build a wonderful relationship but also to experience a whole new life in which your past is one of your many resources but no longer holds you back or confines your potential.

FLYING

In this dream, you are remembering how to fly. It seems like you used to do this a lot in the past, and you may be a little rusty. After the takeoff, you feel a bit confused. Are you supposed to hold your arms out in front or off to the sides, like a bird? As soon as you think about how high you're getting, you may start to lose altitude. But then, when you think positively, you start to soar again. There is a trick to it, all right. You assume a strong position, think confidently about where you want to go, don't look down, and enjoy the rush of the wind in your face.

Flying dreams occur more often during childhood and adolescence and tend to diminish as we mature. When we fly in dreams as adults, it is often because we are experiencing a situation that gives us a feeling of freedom and euphoria. This may relate to self-expression, achievements, or exploration of our interests. Often flying dreams occur when we fall in love or begin a passionate relationship.

Sexual satisfaction and reawakening can trigger flying dreams.

If you are in the early stages of an intimate relationship, the implication of the dream is that you are savoring a sensual chemistry that works well for you. There is also an emotional component to that chemistry—hot sex without feeling does not trigger flying dreams. Somehow, the combination of intimacy, great sex, and meeting another person on a variety of levels sets the spirit soaring in the dream state. The implication is that this relationship works well and that you are embracing the pleasure and the promise it brings you.

LOSING TEETH

In this dream, you are feeling around in your mouth with your tongue. You feel a loose tooth, and you can wiggle it with your tongue. Oops! It falls out, and you spit it out into the palm of your hand. Gross. There is more blood than there should be. Without warning, several more teeth fall out and you spit them out. This is horrible! You have to be somewhere, and this isn't going to look good at all. How are you going to take care of this without people noticing that you have lost half of your teeth? When is your mouth going to stop bleeding?

The dream of losing teeth is one of the most common anxiety dreams in North America. It is a theme that most often occurs intermittently between the ages of fifteen and thirty-five. Both women and men experience this dream theme, but it is more common among women. The dream is related to a situation of forced compromise: the dreamer is wrestling with conflict between what is desired and a course of action that seems reasonable or practical. Although the dream may happen in association with a variety of stressors, it often occurs among women who are struggling with relationship issues of unhappiness and compromise. The theme seems to be associated with a conflict between wanting to make a change or a decision and having officially good reasons why you cannot do so right now.

Cara was thoroughly sick of her current relationship and had decided to break it off. But her partner wanted to take her on a luxury vacation (perhaps in the hopes of rekindling their affair). She told me that she intended to go on the vacation, because it sounded like great fun, but that she would break up with him when they got back. At the time she was making this plan, she was also having recurring dreams of discovering that one of her teeth was rotten and falling out. When we talked about this, she laughed and said that she knew she was not being fair, to the man or to herself, in going on the vacation. She felt this was likely the source of her dreams of losing teeth.

Often the severity of the tooth loss in the dream matches the severity of the emotional wounding the dreamer is experiencing as a result of a compromise. Breeana, who finally escaped from an abusive relationship, told me that during her marriage when she was raising her small children, she often dreamed of her teeth breaking and falling from her mouth. She would be doubled over at the sink, washing all the blood down the drain.

If you dream of losing teeth, consider where in life you are engaged in a situation that goes against the grain with you. Sometimes we make compromises for the best of reasons and do need to stick with something until a process is completed or an obligation fulfilled. When that is the case, though, you need to consider what you can do to bolster your well-being or expand your support system so that the emotional cost of your decision is manageable.

EATING SOMETHING TOXIC

In this dream, you try to eat food that you find distasteful. There may be bugs on the food or maybe it is a dish made from something you would never choose to eat. You may be aware that the food is somehow toxic to you, or you may have a flash of awareness as you eat that you will not be able to keep the food down—that if you keep eating, you will be sick in a few minutes.

In dreams, eating represents the taking in of an experience. We take in life experiences and hopefully find them nourishing in some way. To dream of eating something you cannot tolerate or something that is toxic or poisonous suggests an ongoing experience that is emotionally toxic to you.

Nancy was involved with a man whose teenage kids were acting out. She dreamed that she was at the dinner table with his family and eating rotten meat. With each mouthful, she suppressed her gag reflex and swallowed hard to keep down the revolting taste. She began crying as she ate and finally announced to them all, "I can't do this anymore!"

She had been in an emotional bind. Even though she didn't like his kids or their behavior, she had been taught that if you love someone, you are morally obligated to share that person's problems and take on that person's situation without question. But for her, the family situation was not a welcome addition, and she felt saddled with a toxic life! Because of her belief that being a good person meant accepting her boyfriend's family roller-coaster ride, she had been struggling to swallow the fact that she really did not want this situation for herself. The dream helped her realize that she had been applying standards to her fledgling relationship that were more suitable to an existing marriage and that she had been beating herself up for her feelings. She was not a bad person because she felt that the situation was not what she wanted for her future.

If you dream of trying to eat something that is sickening to you, it is likely that you are trying to take in something that is emotionally toxic to you. Unfair expectations that you are placing on your shoulders may compound the degree of difficulty you have. If this seems true for you, this is a good time to air your feelings with a friend or even a therapist to get some objective input. We seldom dream of eating poison without just cause—if you are trying to take in an experience that is bad for you, it is time to find out what exactly is wrong and whether it is a temporary crisis or a sign of something more serious for your consideration.

CELEBRITY COUPLES

In this dream, you are watching a famous celebrity couple as if you were watching an intimate documentary of their lives. You see their secrets and their conflicts, and you know when one of the partners secretly feels unfulfilled or longs to leave the relationship.

Dreams of observing celebrity couples are like bulletins from magazine headlines. On the surface, they don't seem to have any relevance to the dreamer. But in many cases, the dreams are barometers of your own relationship (or your feelings about relationships). We dream of happy couples when we are happy, and we dream of famous breakups when we are losing momentum in a relationship.

Celebrity dreams about couples can provide you with a way of seeing your own relationship and the challenges you may be facing. Sometimes it is tempting to play the blame game or to just feel fed up and overwhelmed without really being clear about what is bothering you. If you see what is going on between two famous people, you may be getting a clearer emotional vision on your own feelings and what is happening in your relationship. With this clarity, in addition to your instincts about what is going on beneath the surface, you will be able to make decisions wisely. Pay attention to the themes and actions that emerge in your dream of a celebrity couple. Sometimes it is easier to see the mistakes others make, the way they deny their own happiness, or the way they betray one another.

RESPONDING TO YOUR DREAM

We all want fast answers to our relationship questions. Is this something we should invest in emotionally, and is this person going to be a wonderful partner or a waste of time? The bottom line of most relationship dreams is revealed in the underlying theme: connection, discovery, celebration, self-acceptance, recognition, healing, and promise. When we are having conflict or crisis in love, the themes of our dreams can shift to accidents, loss, abandonment, physical ailments, or betrayal.

Although a single dream can provide a critical wake-up call, the dream is best evaluated in the setting of your overall view of the relationship and your feelings about your well-being. Most of us know when we are unhappy or when we are falling in love. Our dreams corroborate those feelings and underscore them in a way that increases our trust and awareness of the movements of the heart. Here are a few suggestions on how to respond to your relationship dream:

· Be honest with yourself about what you have noticed.
· Don't clobber or attack your partner with the content of your dream.

- Weigh the input of your dream carefully, but don't be irrationally impulsive. Consider whether the dream's message falls in line with what you have been sensing in other ways.
- Note whether you have been having a series of dreams that suggest the same message in different ways. If so, the dreams may affirm your conclusions.
- Remember to never attack another person's dignity and to try to be kind, even if you decide to leave a relationship.
- If you are in a new and promising relationship but feel vulnerable, give yourself time. Changes may happen overnight, but adjusting to those changes takes time.
- If you are in a situation that requires time and effort to change, make plans for your future. Enlist friends in your plan and make small adjustments. When you make a decision inside, you will suddenly find ways to make it happen on the outside.
- If you are dreaming of love but are not in a relationship, open up to love in other ways. Embrace your interests, investigate your passions and enthusiasms, take classes, and follow your bliss. By opening your spirit to love and freely giving and receiving on that wavelength, you will be more magnetic and in tune with love when it does cross your path. Don't simply struggle to find a person so that you can experience love. Experience love, and opportunities will surround you.

SYMBOLS IN YOUR DREAMS

When we fall in love, it can seem as if every element of the universe is speaking to us about our relationship. Every song on the radio, every slogan on a bumper sticker, and every book falling open seem to point to something uncannily related to what we are feeling. The landscape of your dreams is like that, too: the setting, the time of day, the weather, and the other people in it can all offer information about your relationship. The weather in a dream, for example, often reflects something about the emotional climate of your current situation, whereas the quality of pleasantness or difficulty in the setting itself can reflect the degree of struggle you are feeling in making the relationship work.

As you have seen by now, the meaning of most dreams is revealed in the central theme and action. Yet there are certain elements in dreams that are highly symbolic, and it is useful to have a sense of the meaning they may hold. Most symbols can have both positive and negative implications; the tone of the dream as well as the way the symbol is presented will make it easy for you to determine which quality the image suggests.

For example, one woman dreamed of sliding down a steep embankment and feeling she might go over the edge. She was in the midst of a breakup that made her feel insecure about her living arrangements as well as her love life. Another woman dreamed of riding down a hill in a go-cart, lifting her feet off the ground, and feeling almost as if she could fly. She had finished a project and was going off with her husband on a vacation. The dream of the downhill ride was, for her, a celebration of an effortless joyride. Both women were dreaming of the downhill symbol, but one was seeing the negative potential, the loss of control; the other was seeing the positive potential of the easy downhill ride.

Exploring Symbols

It is a natural reaction to focus on a single element in a dream and wonder what it could mean. Sometimes the instinct to focus on a single image is wise, particularly if it seems odd or if it repeats. Here are some ways to think about the symbols in your dreams:

- If an image seems out of context, for example, if you're flipping pancakes with a sword, it is likely that exploring the meaning of that symbol is worthwhile. An incongruous item is there deliberately and is part of the symbolic language for expressing something specific.
- If the same item appears in several dreams, whether dead bodies or hummingbirds, you should assume that it is a symbol for something specific in your experience.
- The most common meaning of an item is a loose metaphor for how it is actually used or what it actually does. A scalpel is an incisive instrument that often represents precise logic. An eagle soars high and sees from a great distance, and sometimes represents the power of a high perspective. There is almost always a connection between the everyday reality of the symbol and what it tends to mean in dreams, but the connection is a loose one.

SIGNS OF RELATIONSHIP-THEMED DREAMS

If you are with your partner in a dream, this is an obvious hint that you are dreaming about your relationship or something that the two of you are experiencing together. In some dreams, you may recognize some of the symbols listed in this chapter, but it can be less apparent whether the dream is focused on your relationship or on some other situation in your life. Here are a few telltale signs that will help you to recognize a relationship theme, even if it is not obvious. If even one of these markers from these descriptions was present, and you feel intuitively that the dream was about your relationship, then it is likely a relationship dream. If you are not in a relationship presently, you may still be dreaming about your relationship patterns, and these clues are still valuable for recognizing such themes. Here are some of the typical markers of a relationship-focused dream:

- Your partner appears in the dream, even briefly.
- An old flame is present in the dream.
- A celebrity leading-man type is present in the dream.
- A lover whom you do not know in waking life (such as a fictional character) appears in the dream.
- In different dreams on the same night, you were focused on your relationship and dreamed of your loved one.
- You feel sure, intuitively, that your overriding concern on the night of the dream was your relationship—it was in the forefront of your mind as you went to sleep.
- When you awoke from the dream, your partner or your relationship was the first thing that flashed into your mind.
- There was a committed couple in the dream action (even if they were fictional).
- One of your friends' partners or husbands was present, and you seemed to be involved with him.
- One of your partner's relatives was present, and you seemed to be involved with or having an affair with him.
- There is a dream reference to a famous love affair in history or literature.
- There is a dream reference to couples; marriage; divorce; or people getting together, falling in love, or breaking up.

RINGS

Negative Potential: Rings represent a promise. When you notice something wrong with a ring, this suggests a flaw you have detected in a promise related to the ring. A missing stone, a flawed setting, or something that doesn't fit your taste are common ring defects in dreams. The problem with the ring hints that you sense a problem in the relationship.

Positive Potential: As circles, rings represent the fulfillment of a promise. Within the warmth of a love relationship, we can often complete a goal or retrieve part of our potential that had seemed lost or forgotten. When the ring is pleasing to you, even though it may be modest or unusual, you may have found something beautiful and right for you. You may be involved in keeping a promise to yourself and to the one you love.

WEDDING DRESS

Negative Potential: The wedding dress is an expression of your role in the relationship. If the dress is tattered, horribly flawed, or gruesomely colored, there is something going on that is a mismatch with your hopes for the future.

Positive Potential: When the dress is pleasing to you, this suggests that you are feeling comfortable in your role in the relationship and at ease with your future. The dress might not be for everyone, but why would you want a cookie-cutter relationship? What matters is what makes you happy, and a delightful wedding dress is a symbol of satisfaction with where you are and where you are going.

BED

Negative Potential: The bed is the scene of intimacy in many dreams, and it also is associated with sleep, rest, and privacy. If your bed is in a setting that does not afford privacy, this suggests you may need more space for yourself or more privacy. If your bed is in a strange setting or if you are sleeping at an odd time in the dream, then the implication may be that you are asleep in the metaphorical sense. It may be time to wake up and look with clear eyes at the situation and at how you really feel.

Positive Potential: The bed can be a place of euphoric sensuality and intimacy. If your dream is positive and joyful, and the bed is an appropriate fixture, the bed is likely underscoring the shared happiness of mutual chemistry and closeness.

KITCHEN

Negative Potential: The kitchen in the home represents the sense of family you carry with you. When you are in a kitchen that is barren, bizarre, or unsettling, this implies that you are involved in a situation that should feel good but is in some way disturbing. One woman dreamed that her boyfriend would not come with her into her kitchen. He stood in the doorway as if there were an invisible barrier preventing him from coming inside. She felt that in their relationship she always had to go into his world for them to be together and that he had little ability to join her in her interests or hopes for their future.

Positive Potential: A happy kitchen in your dreams is a hopeful sign of the potential for family-like closeness and blossoming intimacy. Because we cook in the kitchen, it is also associated with the fruitfulness of relationships and the way that good chemistry and closeness can make all facets of life richer and more rewarding.

BASEMENT

Negative Potential: Basements are associated with feelings that are below the surface of conscious awareness or that are not readily apparent. If you dream of something unwholesome or scary in the basement, and you believe the dream is associated with your relationship, then you may be starting to register something subtle that has been bothering you.

Positive Potential: Sometimes basements are settings where we discover a possibility, such as a perfectly good furnace or a hearth where a lovely, cozy fire burns. If you make a wonderful discovery in a basement, the implication is that you and your partner are growing closer and that you have discovered something welcoming and promising in the depths of that closeness.

ATTIC

Negative Potential: Attics often symbolize the haunted places in our hearts where we have stored old pain and fear. Many women dream of frightening attics filled with spiders and creepy things. When attics are associated with relationships, the implication is that you are struggling with feelings that are throwing you back into scary places from the past. This imagery is not necessarily an indictment of the relationship, but it may be time for you to explore what kind of ghosts are haunting you by considering them in the light of day.

Positive Potential: An attic is generally at a high point in the home. For this reason, it may be associated with stored wisdom or potential, the power of secrets honored or promises kept. If the attic is a sacred space to you, then you may be in a process of integrating old and new. Discovering old treasures stored in the attic or clearing it for a new use are themes that bode well for the way you are approaching your current situation.

WINDOWS

Negative Potential: Windows represent a point of view. When windows have a flaw that makes it hard to see clearly (such as when they are cracked, dirty, stained, or damaged), this suggests seeing things from a warped point of view. One woman dreamed that she was looking outside from her parents' window, which was dirty and so old that she could hardly see what was outside. She had been evaluating her relationship from their perspective, and the dream implied that she should consider a more updated and personal point of view.

Positive Potential: Often the windows in our dreams permit us to see a great distance, to see with astonishing clarity, or to witness something of unique beauty. One woman who had gone through a painful breakup dreamed that she got up early and watched the dawn through her bedroom window. The sky was illuminated with spectacular color and light, and the horizon grew clearer and brighter as the sun rose. She knew when she awoke that she was experiencing a beginning, a new day in her life. Although she still had some grief about the past, the dream helped her to embrace the new chapter of her life that was on the horizon.

DOORWAYS

Negative Potential: Doorways symbolize possibilities. If you dream that you let an intruder through the door of your home, it is likely that in some sense you are feeling invaded or even exploited. One woman was trying hard to please her new lover, who seemed to be rather demanding. Yet because she had not been in a relationship for quite a while, she was jumping through hoops to try to please him. She dreamed that she answered the door and that her new roommate, a foreign exchange student, was there. The student was a small, undernourished girl, who was from some foreign land where she had been kept as a slave girl. The girl was so downtrodden that she could not make eye contact or speak for herself. This scene helped the dreamer recognize that she had gotten carried away trying to please her boyfriend and that she needed to keep track of her own well-being and make it a higher priority.

Positive Potential: If you move through a doorway in a dream, you are likely accepting a new chapter in your life. When doorways hold promise, there is often a pleasing change in the way you feel when you cross through them, and there may even be a pleasant change in the lighting or the atmosphere of the place in which you emerge.

WATER

Negative Potential: Water may be associated with emotion, particularly in dreams associated with romance. When the water is tempestuous, the implication is of churning and deep feelings. If water appears because of a leak or flooding and has a dirty quality, then it may be associated with a sense of emotional flooding or of dealing with complex emotional issues that make everything more complex. The more toxic or foul the water, the more likelihood there is that you are dealing with a combination of negatives that make your ability to process and sort through things more difficult.

Positive Potential: Water is healing, nourishing, and restorative when it appears as clear and beautiful. A peaceful body of water suggests a healthy and restorative situation that soothes you. Even a rapid river that demands your attention can be a good sign as long as the tone of the dream is positive and enjoyable.

FOREST

Negative Potential: If a forest is baffling and you feel lost in your dream, it suggests you are having trouble navigating some problems. It is easy to lose your bearings when you lose track of the landmarks you usually rely on. Typically, at the height of our challenges, we dream of getting lost in the woods. We tend to emerge from the forest when we feel at last that we are metaphorically out of the woods. We tend to dream of dark woods when dealing with something on an individual level, so it may be that something in your relationship is triggering a challenge for you.

Positive Potential: The forest is a place of transformation in a symbolic sense. If you find a guide in the forest or are able to find your way out or to a place of safety, then this suggests that you are dealing effectively and courageously with difficulties you have faced. You may have gone through a rough period and emerged strengthened by it.

OCEANFRONT

Negative Potential: The shore is the edge of your personal territory. It is the place beyond which you cannot go. If you are at the shore in a dream and your relationship has been a source of pain, then it is possible that you will take a stand in some way. This is the edge, the boundary, of your heart. Many people dream of going to the shore when they end one chapter of their lives and are opening to what comes next.

Positive Potential: The oceanfront can symbolize what is unlimited. The place where the ocean meets the shore is a place of great promise and healing. The solid ground of the shore can symbolize what we know, what we think, what we believe: the conscious mind. The ocean can symbolize the unlimited psyche and the potency of emotion. The internal territory where these forces unite is a place of immense beauty and power in your spirit. If your relationship has brought you to the oceanfront and the dream is positive, then the implication is both powerful and promising.

Weather as Emotional Climate

Often dreams set the action in the midst of a specific type of weather. This weather may coincide with your current real-life weather, but more often it is associated with the symbolic meaning that the weather holds. Here are the broadest interpretations of what the weather in your dream implies.

SUNSHINE

Sunny times suggest good times, and when sunshine is associated with romance, it suggests a time of promise, easy progress, and rewarding associations. When you are happy and everything makes sense, you are likely to have dreams set in sunny situations.

RAIN

Rain can symbolize sadness or even tears. Often difficulties in relationships are explored in dreams where you are caught in the rain or in which rain falls on the action of the dream.

STORMS

Storms symbolize emotional storms. These can be because of circumstance, but sometimes they are related to stormy personalities or a tendency toward drama or anger. Windstorms symbolize rage and destruction, and wind and water together suggest a combination of angry words and angry feelings.

SNOW

Snow is associated with endings or symbolic death. During the end of a relationship, we often dream of snowy landscapes or of snowfall.

DROUGHT

A lack of emotional support or feeling can create a landscape of drought in a dream. One woman described her marriage as "a long walk in the desert." For her, the dry landscape was like her emotional nature, starved for what it craved.

FOG

Fog makes it hard to see what is right in front of you. Typically, this implies a confusing mixture of feelings and influences, which when combined serves to make it hard for you to see clearly or to know what you feel.

Time of Day

The time of day in which your dream is set may be important. If there is a particular scene in the dream when you observe what time it is, or if the dream is particularly specific about the time of day, it may be useful to consider the general implication of that time.

MORNING

Morning is a time of newness, and it implies the beginning of a chapter in your life. People typically dream of dawn when they are experiencing something new or when the mind is trying to remind them that the end of one chapter can also be the beginning of something new and exciting.

TWILIGHT

Sundown and twilight are times when the day draws to a close. This can be comparable to the ending of a relationship or to when a relationship changes considerably and becomes based on a different footing.

NIGHTTIME

When dreams are set at nighttime, the implication is that we are dealing with something that is challenging to understand and may have an element of mystery. If this makes sense, then night may be a time when you make better use of your intuition than your power of logic.

Your Body as a Dream Symbol

Your dreams often use your body to express or illustrate experiences that affect you in waking life. A wounding word or deed in waking life may appear in a dream as a cut, a nasty bee sting, or the attack of a wild animal. One reason dreams are sometimes gross, violent, or strange is the tendency for your body to be the symbol of whatever is happening in your life. Here are some of the ways in which you may see your body in dreams as a map of your recent experiences.

HAIR

Hair is associated with your thoughts and perspective. Hairstyles are often altered in dreams, reflecting a different mood or perspective. Women often dream of glorious or pleasing hairstyles when they are experiencing something positive that makes them feel good or think positively. Matted, tangled, unkempt, or wild hair suggests that the dreamers are experiencing negativity or confusion in a way that may be running away with them.

FACE

Women often dream about their own faces. Typically, there is some flaw or some new attribute that they notice in the mirror during a dream. Sometimes there is a problem such as a blemish or a rash that the dreamer finds unattractive and embarrassing. She is burdened with wondering how to heal her problem and with embarrassment about it. The face can represent your social identity; it is the thing that others see when they look at you, and it is the self you present to the world. When you feel burdened by your social obligations or that you are on display, you may be more inclined to explore this tension in dreams that feature problems or perceived flaws on or around your face.

HEAD

The head is symbolic of conscious thoughts, logic, and identity. Dreams of damage to the head can reflect damage to self-esteem or to your sense of identity. Dreams of injury to the head are more common among men than women, but when they occur you should view them thoughtfully. A change to the head may reflect a change of mind, while a wound to the head implies a wound to the way you think, to your ideas, or to your point of view.

NECK AND THROAT

The neck is symbolic as the part of you that connects your ideas (your head) with your actions in the world (your body). Problems with your neck in dreams can reflect trouble with tensions that are unique and private. If you feel held back by authority or conflicted in a relationship, you may have trouble with your neck in dreams. Problems with the back of the neck, like the hair on the back of your neck, are associated with instinct and with anger.

The throat is symbolic of your voice and expression. Particularly in relationships, there seems to be an unspoken expectation of what one can and cannot express, or just how much of yourself is welcome. If your authority or creative voice is an issue for you, then that is likely to arise within the context of your relationship, too. If you dream of an injury to your throat, it is possible that you feel constrained against using your voice or being fully yourself.

SHOULDERS

Shoulders can represent power and the ability to take on responsibility. The phrase "broad shoulders" has been used in reference to someone who can handle a great deal of responsibility. In a dream, if you experience a wound to a shoulder, you likely have experienced a slight to your sense of authority or a wound to your vision of yourself as someone who is dedicated and able to cope.

ARMS

Arms can represent your power to extend your gifts to the world, in terms of work and contribution, as well as your ability to hold and embrace love. An injury to the arm in a dream can reflect the experience of feeling separated from someone precious or damage to your sense that you can make a significant contribution of which you can be proud.

HANDS

Hands are an important symbol to men and women, but they most often have significance in the dreams of women. Hands are associated with the power to create, to bring your vision and your intention to life. When you dream of damage, injury, or illness involving the hands, you may be registering a kind of invisible damage to your spirit. Situations that place women in subservient or degrading roles, or that degrade a woman's perspective, often give rise to shocking dreams of violence to the hands. One woman dreamed that when she went to get her engagement photos taken, there was a freakish accident and her hands were cut off. She was struggling with the sense that her dominating partner was diminishing her, even as he superficially showered her with attention. The dream suggested that her upcoming marriage might be a source of loss to her individual power and expression.

SKIN

The skin is the interface, and the boundary, between you and the world. Your skin is the part of you that others see when they look at you. It also registers irritation and sensitivity. When you dream that something is wrong with your skin or that there is an injury or illness visible on your skin, you may be struggling with a situation where a relationship or a social factor is bothering you. Whether you discover a bruise, a nest of spiders hidden in a blemish, or a thorny vine growing from your heel, you not only may be alarmed but also wish to conceal the problem! There is a peculiar vulnerability and shame associated with our dreams of skin problems, and in these dreams, there is sometimes a lack of compassion toward one's own struggle. If you are in a bind of some sort, you can help yourself sort things out more quickly by refraining from judging your own reactions and your needs.

BACK

The back is symbolic of the things that are hidden from direct view. We talk about getting stabbed in the back when we refer to a betrayal that was executed outside of our awareness. When there is a problem with your back in a dream, you may be processing some issue that is happening in the background. Something may be happening that is subtle yet powerful, or it may be that someone is hurting you without even being conscious they are doing so.

THIGHS

Thighs have a sexual connotation. Injuries to the thighs are common in dreams, and they sometimes relate to a sexual wound that has occurred earlier in life. Intimacy, of course, brings us back full circle to issues of trust and fear of being hurt either emotionally or physically.

GENITALS

When women dream of peculiar wounds or conditions around their genitals, this may reflect feelings of vulnerability. Many young women report dreams in which they have a penis or both male and female genitals. Typically, these dreams relate to the way we all process both male and female energy and abilities in our lives.

FEET

The feet and lower legs are associated with our foundation in life and our ability to be mobile. Often relationships alter our sense of where we stand, and they also may affect our sense of freedom. For these reasons, we may dream of something happening to the feet, or even of getting a foot transplant. In general, if a part of the body is wounded, this may mean that there is an emotional wound. When there is a transplant in a dream, this is more often associated with a profound change that has taken place.

Other Themes and Images in Relationship Dreams

VEHICLES

The vehicle in your dream may be a spaceship, a boat, a train, plane, bus, or car. Any vehicle in which you travel with your partner can symbolize your relationship or the journey you are currently on together. The hazards you encounter on your journey tend to represent the impediments you confront as you aim for happiness and fulfillment, both individually and together.

SEPARATION

Often in dreams there is a circumstance or some drama encountered that forces you to separate from your loved one. When this happens, it often reflects a sense of emotional separation that you are experiencing in the relationship. One woman dreamed of a flood that ripped through her hometown. She got on a raft with the kids while her husband got on another raft and floated away from her. In waking life, she was struggling with the knowledge that he was having an affair with a co-worker. Even though her friends all advised her to leave him, she didn't want to do so. She still loved him and wanted the children to have their family intact. The flood was her grief and pain; the separation seemed like the unwanted by-product of the natural disaster that had hit their home life. Yet she weathered the storm, and they mended their marriage, happily, and have been together without trouble for decades.

MUD OR QUICKSAND

Mud, quicksand, and bogs are common in dreams, particularly when dealing with situations that confuse us and make it difficult to get traction. Mud is a combination of earth (which symbolizes logic or conscious thinking) and water (which symbolizes emotion or feelings). Often when we combine these two things, we get a situation that makes us feel uneasy or conflicted. If you are dreaming of mud or getting stuck in quicksand, you are likely dealing with a situation in which you have a strong opinion about what you should do and an equally strong feeling about what you want to do.

When thoughts and feelings are in conflict, we get bogged down. In relationships, often one person is prone to decisions and behaviors based on logic while the other person trusts the gut and has a fine sense of emotional wisdom. When these two people (who each trust their own style of meeting challenges and knowing what is right) are in conflict about a mutual choice, the difference in their styles may paralyze them. If this happens, each person can benefit by acknowledging that the other is processing the question in the manner he or she knows best and that each style is vital to the decision-making process.

TRAVELING UPHILL

The uphill climb in dreams is associated with an effortful enterprise. When we move upward, there is often a worthwhile goal, but the process involves work and effort. During periods of intense work or struggle, you may dream of trying to climb upward with your companion. Frequently in uphill dreams, there is an environmental challenge, such as a slippery surface that makes it harder to get traction. Sometimes there is difficulty with the method you use for climbing, such as trying to drive your car up a flight of stairs. When the approach you use makes the climb harder, this suggests that your waking life behavior is somehow making your progress more difficult.

Some people approach every worthwhile goal, including their relationships, as a battle that is bound to be tough. They slog ahead bravely with furrowed brows and grim determination. They often partner with more lighthearted souls who quietly wonder, "Why does she make everything so hard?" If you dream of a difficult upward climb, don't be afraid to change your approach, pacing yourself, slowing down, or rewarding small victories along the way.

ALWAYS LOOK FOR THE BOTTOM LINE OF YOUR DREAMS

If you did not find your dream in this chapter, you can still make sense of it by stepping back from the story line and identifying the bottom line. Was it a disaster, a surprise happy ending, or an ordeal that you had to face with your lover? Did your behavior and reaction make things better or worse? Although some dreams are more revealing and powerful than others, all your dreams show you two things: what is going on and how your responses are working for you. Don't be overwhelmed by a complex or unusual story line, just look for the bottom line and how your role in things affects the result.

Symbols Represent Functions

If you have a symbol in your dream that you cannot find information on, ask yourself what function the object serves in the broadest sense. Objects in dreams are associated with functions, and those functions typically have an emotional equivalent. For example, doctors use sutures to close a wound so it can heal. The function is closure and healing. If you dream of having an injury stitched by a doctor, the emotional equivalent is reacting to your pain in a way that keeps you safe and helps you heal.

If a symbol still does not make sense, you can describe it out loud by putting the word *emotional* or *personal* in front of it as you paraphrase the dream. For example, if you are in a boating accident in your dream, it might not make sense at first. But if you say, "My emotional boat is sinking," you may have a quick flash about what this means about your relationship or the situation in question. If you dream that a man is following you with a knife, you may not have a feeling for what that means. However, if you say, "A man threatens me with an emotional weapon," you will then click into what the dream is reflecting. If you dream of a dried-up garden suddenly blooming, you might say, "My personal garden is coming to life."

Using simple techniques to get clarity from a dream does not mean that you have reduced, diminished, or disrespected the profound wisdom of the dream. It is merely an approach for entering the intersection between thinking and knowing in which the wisdom of dreams is more accessible. Once you crack a dream's meaning, you will start to see additional elements in it that are familiar and revealing to you as well.

Chapter 10

LISTENING TO YOUR SUBCONSCIOUS

*Program Your Dreams and Hear the
Intuitive Wisdom of Your Heart*

People often ask if there is any way to direct their dreams toward the people or situations they would like to dream about. Some people are very gifted in this area and can easily influence their dreams. But the rest of us can learn to direct our dreams, too: the process is often called dream incubation or dream programming.

Your dreams are always focusing on what is going on in your life, what you desire, and what you are trying to avoid. When you program your dreams in a specific direction, you are merely accelerating the process and targeting the kind of information that you are most interested in discovering. I've been using this process and sharing it with others for many years, and it is easy to learn. Some people love it and make it almost a habit, but others find it more useful as a technique they can call on when they want some particular insight. After my experiences with listening to meditation recordings before taking naps, and the precognitive dreams they triggered, I can assure you that what we do and think about just prior to sleep can have very powerful results.

The Dream-Programming Technique

Focus: Focus your attention on the topic you want to dream about. You can think about it, journal your thoughts, or chat with someone else about your interest. Just dwell on the topic prior to sleep.

Question: Create a simple, short question that sums up what you want to know.

Repeat: As you drift off to sleep, silently repeat the question over and over. If possible, match part of the question to your inhalation and part to your exhalation. If your question is brief, you may be able to repeat it with each inhalation and exhalation. Don't drive yourself crazy with this; just try to do it in a relaxed manner so that it doesn't interfere with your ability to drift off to sleep.

Record: Have something readily available by your bed so that when you wake up you can record the dream you have had.

Your dreaming mind is capable of responding to your inquiry the first time, particularly if you are a vivid dreamer. However, it may take a few tries before you feel you have gotten satisfactory results. If you have a problem or can't remember your dream, then ask again in a night or two. Also, feel free to approach this in the manner that suits you best. Some people go all out and meditate, say a prayer, or listen to special music before falling asleep to get in the mood. Others hop into bed, focus their mind, come up with a question, and start inhaling and exhaling to the question all very quickly and with no fuss.

What should you ask? Whatever you want to know. If you are currently in a relationship and feel that you're missing something or that it just isn't clicking, you could ask to be shown what you're missing in the relationship. If you are interested in meeting someone special, you might ask what you could do to prepare for love or where you could look to meet your mate. Some people ask how they can bring more love into their lives.

If you have been working for some time on an issue and have not been getting much traction, then dream programming might be just the thing to get you past the logjam. If you already know what you want and how you should be able to get it, and you have been watching yourself not make it happen, then there may be something else going on. One extremely potent approach is to ask your dreams, "What do I need to take care of before I can accomplish this?" Typically, with effective people who know what they want and can't make it happen, there is a piece of the puzzle that they have not taken care of that prevents them from crossing the finish line.

CLEARING THE PAST

Information about old hurts or bitter feelings that have not been released frequently appears in programmed dreams about relationships. When we are traumatized or disappointed, the pain usually goes one of two ways: it turns into anger or fear. Anger bubbles up with a life of its own, protecting us from getting hurt again and making others behave themselves, too. Fear causes us to alternate between hyperactive agendas and social paralysis. If you are not progressing toward your goals in a way that seems reasonable, start clearing the past. You may need to forgive someone or forgive yourself. You may need to talk things out with a friend or therapist. Give yourself room and time to let things go! This doesn't mean you will forget or that you will condone bad conduct. It simply means that you won't bind yourself to the scar tissue of that old wound anymore. Your emotions will circulate normally instead of getting routed down the same old detour that leads to the same dead-end street.

If you don't feel like forgiving or if it just seems like a wimpy concept to you, turn the process over to your deeper mind. There is a part of you that knows how to forgive, and you can let that part of you do the forgiving. It is that simple. You may even want to use this statement: "There is a part of me that knows how to forgive, and I let that part of me do the forgiving now. I am free." If a formerly painful situation comes to your mind, just make that statement and move on to the next thing.

There are many wonderful books and journals available on the process of forgiveness. If you enjoy working with others or you want to explore this idea further, you may want to look into them. Forgiveness is something that requires very little time, money, or action—it is an emotional and psychological release. Yet forgiving is one of the most important things you can do for yourself, and it can completely transform your life.

MEDITATION

If you want to become more grounded in your brilliant sanity and connect with the wisdom of your dreams and intuition, meditation can be immensely helpful. You may want to try a recorded guided meditation or seek out a recording by your favorite self-help author. If nothing else, take fifteen minutes every other day and lie down to listen to relaxing music and let your mind envision what you want most or what you find soothing. Meditation builds a bridge between your deeper mind and your conscious thoughts so that they are no longer so separate. The result of this connection is heightened intuition, clearer awareness of what is true and important, and a calming of emotional swings. You will remember your dreams better and will find that you can direct your dreams more easily when you choose to do so.

Minute Meditations

If you don't know where to start with meditation and feel you don't have time to deal with one more thing, two meditation statements follow that you can read out loud when you are alone. After you read one, sit quietly for a minute and simply breathe, letting the statement sink in. You can keep these meditations at your desk, and take a moment now and then throughout the day to read one, breathe for one minute, and then get back to work. You can also write your own meditation statements and use them the same way or find affirmations or prayers others have written, write them on an index card, and keep one in your purse. Repeated statements are powerful and effective, and they cost nothing to use.

Inviting Love

I am ready to receive love in my life and to enjoy a loving partnership. I let go of the past and prepare my heart for mature, unselfish love that will uplift and nourish both parties. I welcome the right partner into my life and trust I will know that person clearly and calmly when he crosses my path. I am making my life ready to share. My brilliant sanity helps me see clearly and make wise choices; I am in the right place at the right time, and my spirit is light. If that person is somewhere and has been waiting for a sign, this is the sign. Come now.

Letting Love Blossom

I make room in my heart for the love I have with this person to blossom and grow. I allow this connection to flourish and to be only wholesome and good. I send kind thoughts to this person throughout the day, and I remember to be kind to myself as well. This need not be forced: love will flourish and grow between us and become richer and stronger with time. I come from a place of peaceful joy and warmth. My thoughts and feelings are like the sun, the air, the water, and the earth: if this is love, it will grow.

THE INTUITIVE WISDOM OF YOUR HEART

Imagine that you can move your consciousness into the center of your heart. There exists a place of deep compassion, wisdom, and understanding of what is true for you and what is happening with others. From this place, the truth does not hurt; you warmly understand it, accept it, and act upon it with decency and compassion. Relationship intuition that becomes available to you when you move your consciousness into your heart energy is the intuition that is related to your connections with others, your love of family and friends, your affection for everything in life you cherish. The wise intuition of your heart is so clear that you can move into it any time you feel overwhelmed with the complexity of a situation or when forces are pulling you in different directions.

Ask the Heart about Love

Your physical sensations and the mood of your body are closely linked with the deep wisdom of your intuition. The sensations around the heart, as well as the emotional feeling associated with the heart, are particularly in tune with your relationships and with the truth about what makes you happy. Here is the process for checking in with the wisdom of your heart:

- Get comfortable and quiet. You will want to do this alone, or at the very least with friends who are interested and approach it sincerely.

- Imagine that you can move your consciousness into a room in the center of your chest that is spacious and warm. This is a

space where you understand, where you are safe and beyond ideas of right and wrong, where the love is boundless.
· Imagine that you can dwell in this space, and as you breathe in and out, it becomes more real and defined.
· From this place of heart energy, ask your question. See and experience whatever arises in response to the answer. Be gentle and patient, allowing the experience to come to you. Take your time.
· When your process feels complete, come back to your normal state. You may want to jot down notes about what happened or simply digest what you experienced.

Using your imagination to move your feelings into a positive, loving orientation is powerful and effective, even if it isn't something you have tried before. Frequently, students will roll their eyes as I describe an exercise and then look at me, stunned, when it is over. There is nothing magic going on—it is simply that we know so little about the immensity of the wisdom inside us that when we receive a powerful insight, we are shaken that it was apparently right there for the asking.

What Should You Ask?

You can access heart wisdom any time you want to check in with a deeper perspective on a question that troubles you. You can ask about the suitability of a love interest, if you like. Or you can ask about what really was going on in a past relationship. If you are in a perfectly good relationship that just doesn't seem fulfilling, you can ask to better understand the situation. If you are in a relationship with a difficult person, you may be astounded at the insights you can gain about the friction or the feelings involved.

You can ask for guidance on how to handle a relationship better or to move past a difficult passage. Sometimes challenges don't have rapid answers, and you have to stay with something over time. In such a case, you can ask simply to have the energy of your heart be present in your experience in a stronger way in the days to come so that you feel connected and powerful rather than stricken or blank.

Remember, if you feel confused, can't remember why something once seemed important, or know you should care about something but can't find that caring in you, these are all signals that you have been turned around. Your powerful, wise, loving, unshakable heart is right there inside, always, and you can check in there to be reminded of the bigger picture, and the real you.

The inner work described here can support your preparing for love or nourishing of the relationship you already have: program your dreams, clear the past, meditate, feel free to tailor these to suit your time and preferences, and listen to your heart.

Conclusion

*E*veryone wants to find and enjoy love. I get letters and emails from girls of fourteen and from grandmothers of eighty-eight who are touched and encouraged by their dreams of love. Throughout the life span, our preoccupation with seduction and conquest changes, but our urge to love and be loved only grows. With practice, time, and thoughtfulness, our ability to express love and to maintain relationships improves. There is a cultural myth that women seek commitment and men do not, but I have not found this to be true. There are lots of nice, successful, loving men out there who find it difficult to meet someone they can love; they are, if anything, more lonely and discouraged than the women.

If you are single and you want to find someone to love, then you will. It may not be tomorrow, and it may not be quite what you expected, but you will find it. In listening to the stories of happy couples who have been together some time, I have found four points that many of them have in common. Bear these in mind as you move forward.

Love on the rebound is often quite perfect. Many of the happy couples I know met after one person had suffered a broken heart.

I had always heard that people on the rebound were vulnerable and prone to making errors, but there seems to be another factor at play as well. After a rotten time, we take stock. We look back on mistakes or how we tried too hard, or we recognize that the other person had never been as involved as we were. Also, there is a new emotional courage that comes after a desperate disappointment. It is as if the worst has already happened; lightning has already struck; and you are left more honest, open, and caring than before. Also, when you lose someone, there is the sense that your chance for happiness is gone, and so you drop your agenda; you stop projecting and posturing and trying to win the courtship game. Instead, you come from your heart, sobered, tender, and wide-eyed. From this point of sincerity, grief, and simplicity, it is often the case that you run smack-dab into the love of your life. So if you are emerging from a painful ending, do your grieving and take care of yourself, but also trust that life has more to offer you. Be honest, caring, and clear, and you will see the real thing when you encounter it.

Many of the people who found their mate have told me that they went through some soul-searching beforehand and determined that they were ready for love. They didn't just want it; they also felt ready. They also reported that they did some self-reflection about the fact that they were ready for love. Some reported that they prayed and asked a higher power to send them their mate. Others practiced affirmations or declarative statements intensely for a short time and then let go of the issue and got on with their lives. In a relatively short time, they say they met their life partners. It is not clear whether we can conjure or attract love when we want it, although some people give it a good try. However, I believe absolutely that setting your internal permissions, engaging in positive self-talk, affirmations, declarative statements, and prayer (if that is your belief) can be immensely powerful and effective for clearing the psyche for love and empowering you to recognize and meet love when it comes your way.

Those who are happy in love seem to have a knack for balancing their inner wisdom, such as dreams and intuition, with wholesome external action. This balance helps them to know what is right, to feel the rhythm of timing in life, and to take positive steps to help fate along. People who are all action and no insight tend to put a great deal of effort into meeting lots of unsuitable people, sometimes feeling a little discouraged in the process. However, if we spend all our time dwelling on our ideal scenario but refusing to meet anyone new, then we may be out of balance as well. Happy lovers tend to make the most of inner wisdom and outer action, and it seems this is a healthy and effective combination.

Happy couples seem to keep a practice of lifelong learning. They are always reading; studying; and learning about themselves, about their relationship, and about life. This creates a dynamic personality and a flexible, strong relationship. If you like to learn, then reach out for what you want to study. Don't expect all the answers to be in one class or event, but keep exploring and adding wisdom to your set of resources.

Our greatest gifts are the loving hearts and the wise spirits around us. Make it a habit to ask people you admire about their perspectives, what they feel is important to a good relationship, and how they recognized the loves of their lives. Make a plan to share your dreams with interested friends and help one another explore their meaning. Keep some kind of record of your interesting dreams so that you can see for yourself how they parallel your life experiences and express your feelings. Practice listening to your intuition and even asking your deeper mind for some input when you need a fresh point of view.

Have faith in yourself and confidence in your dreams. Your search for and understanding of love will be richly rewarding.

About the Author

Larry Stewart

Gillian Holloway has been teaching about the meaning in dreams for twenty years. She is the author of three other books on dream analysis, and she teaches courses on dream psychology and intuition at Marylhurst University near Portland, Oregon. Her research into modern dream symbols and themes has been written about in many popular publications and has been presented at conferences for the International Association for the Study of Dreams.